Young Superstars of Tennis

of Tennis

The Venus and Serena Williams Story

Young Superstars
of Tennis

The Venus and Serena Williams Story

Mike Fillon

Avisson Press, Inc.
Greensboro

First edition
Printed in the United States of America

Library of Congress Cataloging-in-Publication Data

Fillon, Mike.
Young superstars of tennis: the Venus and Serena Williams story / Mike Fillon.--1st ed. p. cm.-- (Avisson young adult series)
Includes bibliographical references (p.).
Summary: A dual biography of the African American teenaged sisters who are revolutionizing the world of professional tennis with their colorful hair beads, fresh personalities, and growing talent for the game.
ISBN 1-888105-43-7 (lib. bdg.)
1. Williams, Venus, 1980- 2. Williams, Serena, 1981- 3. Tennis players--United States--Biography--Juvenile literature. 4. Afro-American women tennis players--Biography--Juvenile literature. [1. Williams, Venus 1980- 2. Williams, Serena, 1981- 3. Tennis players. 4. Women--Biography. 5. Afro-Americans--Biography.] I. Title. II. Series.

GV994.A1 F54 1999
796.342'092'273--dc21
[B]

99-051981

Frontispiece: Serena, left, and Venus Williams with trophies after Venus defeated her sister in the finals of the 1999 Lipton Championship at Key Biscayne, Florida,

Photo credits: All photos are from AP/Wide World Photos.

Dedication
For my mother, Helen M. "Pat" Fillon

Contents

Introduction

The tennis world will never forget February and March of 1999. That is when two teenage girls who grew up in a California ghetto made sports history.

First, Venus and Serena Williams each won tournaments on the same day, on two different continents; Venus in Oklahoma City and Serena in Paris, France. They quickly followed that feat by meeting in the finals of the Lipton Championship in Key Biscayne, Florida. It was the first time siblings had faced each other in the finals of a tennis tournament in 125 years.

Afterwards, many experts predicted the sisters were poised to take over women's tennis for some time. Said highly-ranked veteran player Jana Novotna, "my feeling is they both will be at the top." Added well known tennis coach Rick Macci, "The question is not if they'll be number one, but who will get there first."

Women's tennis has not seen this combination of sheer power, accuracy and physical stamina since the height of the great Martina Navratilova's career. Yet, the Williams sisters are still teenagers. Throughout tennis history, there have only been a handful of successful African-Americans, including Althea Gibson, Arthur

Ashe, and 1940's pioneer Reginald Weir. But the Williams sisters are special for other reasons, too. They're both supremely confident of their abilities, and of their destinies as superstars of tennis; some would even say they are cocky. Here's a typical Venus Williams comment. You decide:

"I think that in today's world a lot of people are suffering from (a lack of) confidence. And the reason that they can't say that they believe in themselves or what they're going to do is because they really didn't believe it in the first place. . . So, I wouldn't consider myself cocky or arrogant. I consider myself confident, and I tell the truth."

Cocky or not, the Williams sisters are changing women's tennis, possibly with long-term effects for the future of the sport. The confidence has been hard-won. Venus and Serena have worked diligently to rise to the top of the tennis world. The odds were against them from the beginning. The things that carried them from a California ghetto to tennis riches are their faith, family, love, friendship, and education . They've had to learn to deal with both success and failure. Their parents have taught them that education is most important and also to strive to be their best.

They've also been taught to "give something back." Venus and Serena conduct tennis clinics all over the country, usually in poor areas for minority kids.But, do they encourage other children to become tennis champions? Not at all.

"I think it's important to go out there and have a lot of fun," says Serena. "If you're not enjoying what you're doing, it's really hard to do well."

There's more to Venus and Serena than just tennis, and they have proved that they ahve real talent, over and above the hype that has surrounded them. They're different. Here's their story.

Chapter 1:
Beginnings

V enus Ebone Starr Williams was born on June 17, 1980, in Lynwood, California, the fourth of five daughters born to Oracene (also called Brandi) and Richard Williams. Her elder sisters are Yelunde, the oldest, who now plans to become a doctor; Isha, who has studied law; and Lyndrea, who is two years older than Venus. Serena Williams, who later would become a young tennis star in her own right, was born on September 26, 1981, in Saginaw, Michigan– one year, three months and nine days after Venus, she likes to say. The girls' father planned their tennis lives before they were even born. Richard Williams was the only son born to Julia Williams, a field worker and sometime custodian in rural Shreveport, Louisiana in the 1940s. One thing Richard remembers about Shreveport was that, though the races were segregated, they were polite to each other and respecting of those who worked hard and tried to improve themselves regardless of their race. "It didn't matter what color people were where I came from," Williams told the *Palm Beach Post*. He recalls how self-reliance and self-improvement were traits everyone admired. This is the kind of work ethic and respect for others Mr. Williams says he's tried to teach to his daughters. "My daughters don't talk about things like [racism], nor do they even feel things like that," he said. "I brought them up the same way I was brought up. I never felt racism."

Richard and his four sisters never knew their father, who had abandoned their mother. These experiences taught him the importance of the presence of a father for kids. He absolutely loved his mother. Richard Williams said his mother taught him pride, decency, religion, and that the family was the backbone of civilization. "The only mistake she ever made was marrying my father," he told the *New York Times Magazine*. Perhaps because the father was not present, at times the family received welfare. To help make ends meet, Richard made a few dollars throwing out trash for a local doctor.

Once, after a long day in the cotton fields, Richard's mother asked him, "If you had to work this hard all your life, would you like it?" He knew by such lessons that education was the only way out. Although a formal education was beyond his reach, it is a lesson he has drilled into his five daughters all their lives.

Explaining his mother's role in his upbringing, Richard told the *Christian Science Monitor,* "My mom was my hero. My mom was my life. My mom was the greatest person who ever lived. She was happy every day of her life. She taught me what life was about, what giving was about. She told me to be successful, and that I should keep my mouth closed until I have something to say." Richard's mother died in 1985.

Richard was a talented athlete who played baseball, football, basketball, whatever sport was around. Still, he saw no future in Shreveport. While still in his teens, he left Louisiana and moved to Chicago to work construction jobs. He then moved to Watts in Southern California, where he met his future wife, Oracene, at church.

The couple soon got married and had three daughters before Venus was born in 1980. At first, Mr. Williams wanted to name Venus "Winfield Two Horse Hop Grass Williams." That's because, "I thought being born in the ghetto, she'd better learn to be ... as tough as can be." He thought the name would help. Fortunately for Venus, her mother won out and nixed the idea. Oracene gave birth to Serena 15 months later while the family lived in Michigan, Oracene's home state.

Like her husband, Oracene Williams was the oldest child in a large family, though she had seven siblings to Richard's four. She's been nurturing children her entire life. "Since both Richard and I were the oldest, we're both used to being in control," she says. "So that's where we would get a little conflict. I had to learn to back off."

That doesn't mean she holds back her opinions, or

can't put her foot down when necessary. She's even gotten more involved recently in coaching her daughters. She often shouts out comments during practices and offers advice during water breaks. Like any mother, she worries about her children as they embark on their chosen careers.

Richard first became interested in tennis in 1978 after watching a women's tournament on TV. Lounging in a chair, he bolted upright when he heard how much money the winner would receive. He doesn't remember the exact amount of the winner's check, but it was at least double his own salary working an untold number of hours.

"I felt that if someone could go out there and play tennis for about four days and make that type of money, I was in the wrong business," Williams said. That's when he started planning a tennis future for his daughters, not knowing the two youngest would be the ones to carry out his dream. To learn about the game, he watched instructional videotapes by former tennis stars Stan Smith and the late Arthur Ashe. From them, he learned the correct way to hit forehands, backhands, and how to serve. He also starting going to the public library and reading *Tennis* magazine. Richard even talked to psychiatrists and psychologists about a tennis life for his kids.

When Venus was three years old, the family returned to California. Along the way, Richard went to business college and worked at a bank, a department store, and in real estate. Eventually the girls' father opened a janitorial service in Long Beach. He then switched careers and became owner of Samson Security, a small company that hired out security guards. The family moved to Compton, a rough and tumble town on the outskirts of Los Angeles because, as he told the *Christian Science Monitor,* he wanted to go somewhere he was needed.

Afraid for her children's safety, Oracene didn't want to go, but Richard won out. "I thought it would be best to bring my kids up in the ghetto," he has told reporters. "Living in the ghetto you learn that you have to be real tough," and because, "kids from the best neighborhoods don't try so hard."

By 1984, Richard Williams was ready to put into practice his plan to make his two youngest daughters successful. When Venus was four-and-a-half years old and Serena three, Williams took them to the tennis court for the first time. "I knew she [Venus] was a champion right away," he has said. But no one, not even Venus' mother, believed him.

He and the girls would practice on run-down public courts every chance they could – and sometimes couldn't. "I actually had to fight young men to take that tennis court," Richard recalls. "I remember taking them courts and they started shootin' at Venus, Serena, and myself. We had to duck and dodge and crawl like in [Viet] Nam." Compton, California has some 50 youth gangs including many branches of the Crips and Bloods. Eventually, Venus' father made an unusual pact with the gang members. He would help them go back to school if they would guard the court against intruders.

Soon the Williams trio would show up at the court almost daily. The athletically gifted girls would hit tossed tennis balls thousands of times on the hot, cracked courts in Compton. Well, in theory they hit them. At first the girls would swing and miss most of them. Richard remembers Venus lofting only four or five over the ripped net. Still, she wouldn't give up, and her father would admire her determination.

Venus would constantly beg Richard to take her to the tennis courts. Once there, she would beg him to stay. Then, when Venus was five and without warning, her father took away her racquet for over a year. Not because Venus had done anything bad, and not to be mean, but to teach her a valuable lesson. "She was starting to love it too much," her father recalls.

Although Richard wanted Venus to be successful, he realized he was creating a monster. "I wasn't looking to develop a tennis player as much as I was looking to develop a human being ... I'm more interested in having a number one student because that will last a lifetime."

Venus outgrew her extreme love of tennis by spending time doing other things. She and Serena had a normal sibling rivalry as children. Venus later said that Serena "used to be terrible ... She stole things from me." But Serena says that she was six years old the last time she fought with Venus.

Although Venus was dismayed that she temporarily wasn't allowed to play tennis, she spent her time developing other interests, including reading. She never once questioned Richard's decision. "He's my teacher," Venus said, adding that she's never disagreed with anything her father has told her. "Generally, I'm an agreeable person. I like to do what I'm told and set a good example for Serena." When Venus was six years, seven months old, he allowed her back on the court. Over time, Venus developed her rifle-shot serve, often to the ring of gunfire in the neighborhood.

Chapter 2:
"The Ghetto Cinderella"

The area between Bakersfield and San Diego, California has long been known as the cradle of tennis stars. Well-known names from the history of tennis developed their game here, including Jack Kramer, Pancho Gonzales, Billie Jean King, and Stan Smith. Today's sensation, Pete Sampras, also played here.

But a reputation for success like this also breeds problems. In 1992, there were almost 14,000 children officially registered as Junior players in California. More often then not, behind the youngsters were parents pushing them too hard. Besides coaches, some parents also hired nutritionists and personal trainers. Many parents had crossed the line between parental support and parental pressure.

"The parents want to win and win," Richard Williams told the *New York Times* in 1992. "I've never seen a sport where you have to win and win."

But as a young teenager, Venus did win and win, from the first Junior tennis match she ever played. At 5' 4"

Althea Gibson competing during the title match at Wimbledon
in 1957. She defeated Darlene Hard 6-3, 6-2.

inches tall with spindly arms and legs, she could jump
higher, hit harder and cover the court better than her
opponents. Only she did it without pressure from her
parents. For her, it was still fun.

By the time Venus was ten years old, she had become
a Southern California legend, with Serena not far behind
her in either ability or notoriety. Though the younger

daughter trailed behind Venus in sheer ability, the deficit was mostly because she was younger and not as strong. Venus had a tall, willowy strength, while Serena was developing a shorter, compact strength that would later stand her in good stead.

Richard Williams helped spread the news of his promising athletic daughters by hyping their abilities at every opportunity. And there were many willing listeners, including the newspapers and television stations. It's no wonder why. Tales of "ghetto Cinderellas with the golden rackets" had great appeal in a country club sport that had not had more than a handful of black players in the almost 50 years they had been allowed to play professionally.

The history of African-Americans in tennis is short but interesting. In March of 1948, a New York physician, Dr. Reginald Weir, became the first black person to play in a United States Tennis Association (known then as the USLTA – U.S. Lawn Tennis Association) national championship tournament. At the 1950 USLTA National Indoors championships, Ms. Althea Gibson became the first black person to be seeded and the first to reach the final of a national championship tournament. On August 25, 1950, Gibson's twenty-third birthday, history was made as she became the first African American to play in the USLTA National Championships (now known as the U. S. Open). The crowd for Gibson's first-round match against Barbara Knapp was one of the largest ever for the

Arthur Ashe in the third set of his title match against Jimmy Connors at Wimbledon in 1975. Ashe won the crown in four sets.

time. Apredominantly black crowd, they saw Gibson win 6-2, 6-2.

In 1951, before becoming the first black American to play at the prestigious Wimbledon tournament, Gibson won her first international title, the Caribbean Championship, in Montego Bay, Jamaica. Gibson won her first major singles title in 1956 at the French Championships, one of the four Grand Slam tournaments. The bigger breakthrough, however, came the following year when she won Wimbledon. Afterwards, Gibson was given a ticker-tape parade along Broadway in New York

City. She then won the women's singles title at the U. S. National Championships.

The late Arthur Ashe, who died in 1993 from complications from the HIV virus contracted during a blood transfusion, had been one of the top-ranked male players in the world for a number of years; his dignified presence on and off the court had made him a genuine role model for young people. Some of his titles included U.S. Open singles champion in 1968 and Wimbledon singles champion in 1975. He had also won the Australian Open singles championship, and had been a member of the U. S. Davis Cup team for a number of years between 1963 and 1978.

From the age of nine to eleven, Venus Williams drubbed every opponent in the Junior ranks, compiling a 63-0 record. In the extremely competitive Southern California district of junior tennis, she often won her matches 6-0, 6-0. It wasn't long before news about Venus' tennis ability traveled across the country. Jack Kramer, a tennis legend from many years ago, saw her play and proclaimed her a future Grand Slam champion. Zina Garrison, the top black female player at the time, called her the best 10-year-old she had ever seen. Also, *Tennis* magazine ran its first article about her in 1991.

Though Venus was quickly becoming well-known, the younger and less known Serena was nevertheless supportive of her sister in every way. Venus grew to depend on Serena "We help each other out," Venus later said. "I've told Serena, 'When you play, if you can't be there, be there anyway.' She said 'I wasn't there, but I was there anyway.' So she was talking to me before I went out to my match. And sometimes I will say things to her so we help each other out ... So, usually we encourage each other."

Then, Richard and Oracene Williams decided again that the sport was taking up too much of their daughters' time and had both Venus, then eleven, and Serena, then nine, stop playing competitively. The parents decided to have their daughters focus on education first and tennis second.

Critics of the parents' decision said the girls would become better prepared for the pros if they continued to play in Junior events. In the tennis world, junior players mature and develop experience from playing in Junior tournaments. Most top players, such as Monica Seles, Martina Hingis and Jennifer Capriati, played on the Junior tour. For example, in 1993, Hingis became the youngest player to win a Junior title, taking the French Open at the age of 12 to break the record set by 13-year-old Capriati in 1989. But Venus' and Serena's parents stood firm.

Why did Richard and Oracene Williams – once again – do something so unpredictable? From the beginning, the parents, especially the father, have closely supervised the girls' careers making sure they didn't play too much tennis too early. For one thing, the parents worried about injuries. In particular, Richard didn't want injuries caused by playing on hard courts all day. Junior players often suffered from muscle pulls, broken bones, stress fractures, and ligament damage. There were even some who needed surgery on their feet and legs.

Other issues that concerned Mr. and Mrs. Williams were those of burnout and the psychological problems faced by some players. "When you're out there playing all those tournaments, no one is happy out there," Richard Williams said. "Everyone is sad. And I'm not bringing my kids up to be sad kids."

By this time, the parents had had enough of the Junior program. They didn't like how some parents and kids behaved. They saw some parents abuse their own children after they lost to his daughters in tournaments. Richard said he also saw too many parents living through their kids and pushing them to make it. "Then guess what? They don't make it anyway."

Richard Williams says there are "no bad kids" in the world, but there are parents "who are not worth a nickel." Mr. Williams said he told his children they were the best in everything they did, and they believed it. "Something good is going to happen if you learn to stand alone, learn what a work ethic is and have a long-term plan."

He said he saw too many kids not having fun. "You can't make a child grind, grind, grind for six hours. That's a fool that would do that to a kid."

Oracene Williams echoes her husband's sentiments, saying "When I first went to a tournament, all the players looked so sad . . . They look like they hate to be out there, that they're scared. Even the top ones, with the exception of Hingis. They're scared of the competition when they should be inviting it. Venus doesn't worry about winning, because she knows she isn't going to lose."

Also, the parents thought practicing tennis and playing junior tournaments took too much time away from the children's school work and family gatherings. "I couldn't understand how I could get my kid to have a good education and be at the tennis tournament, Saturday and Sunday, and practicing all week, getting ready for it," Mr. Williams said.

Oracene said she wants her daughters to be more than "just tennis players." As a child in Saginaw, Michigan, she had heard stories about famous African-Americans, such as heavyweight champion boxer Joe Louis, left with no money when their careers ended. She sees her and her husband's duty to their children as teaching them values to cope with life and helping them develop the mental toughness to compete in tennis. "In tennis, you have to have a head," Oracene Williams said. "Anything mental will get to you."

The mother is the quiet parent, but also the disciplinarian. "I'm the one who sets the schedule, but I've never had a problem with my girls," she told the *Atlanta Journal & Constitution,*. Among the rules for the girls:

Watch no more than two hours a week of television, have no parties, and go to bed by nine. As for watching tennis matches, there is no clapping "because it don't do no good," said their father.

When they quit playing in the Junior tournaments, the girls didn't give up tennis, just competing. Venus' parents believed their natural will to win would hinder their ability to learn and experiment on the court.

Plus, the girls' father said it was more important for his daughters to spend more time on their school work and to develop interests outside of tennis. Both girls had started taking guitar lessons. Other activities they enjoyed were basketball, rollerblading, surfing, reading, and shopping. They also studied French and Spanish.

At one time, Venus said she hoped to be an astronaut or an archeologist. "Tennis is one of my dreams, but I'm also dreaming of getting a good education so I have something to back my life up with."

But there was still another reason for dropping competition. Venus was just too good. Her parents saw no value in playing opponents she could beat so easily. There were more important things for her to do. Although she didn't play in tournaments, Venus didn't stop playing tennis. Her day included schooling at home as well as practice; she spurned the international junior circuit. Still, her father predicted she would be a Grand Slam champion by 16.

Chris Evert's teenage debut two decades earlier

prompted many other parents to push their children into tennis. The result? Tracy Austin, who became the youngest U.S. Open champion when she was 16-years-old, walked away from the sport soon after due to health problems and the constant pressure. Jennifer Capriati and Andrea Jaeger rocketed to the top of the women's tour as teenagers, but quickly fizzled. A shoulder injury ended Jaeger's career. Capriati, who turned pro at 14, rebelled against the loss of her youth. She was arrested for shoplifting and left the tour for a while after a marijuana charge and entered drug rehabilitation. She is still trying to make a comeback. These are only the ones who made it to the top.

Although many players felt that the girls had hurt their chances of success by stopping their competition in the Junior tournaments, Venus and Serena were able to succeed. By 1991, Jim Hillman, tennis director for the Southern California Tennis Association (SCTA), was getting ten phone calls a week about the Williams girls. Hillman had gotten to know Richard Williams when the father taught briefly for the SCTA in the mid-'80s. He remembers Richard having total control over his daughters but relates that the father wasn't a problem parent during tournaments. Even then, Hillman said Richard stressed education and raising well-rounded children. "But for a girl who didn't play junior tennis, he really kept Venus' name in the papers," Hillman said.

Williams agrees. "I am the best agent there is," he laughed.

Tennis coach Rick Macci was teaching in Haines City when a sports agent told him about "this 10-year-old girl in California" he just had to see. The agent told him she was raw and the family probably couldn't pay him much, but that she had a gift. "I'm not interested," Macci told him. "I hear it all the time: 'I've got the next Jennifer,' and they never do." But when Richard called a few weeks later and asked him to fly to Compton, he became intrigued.

"All I can guarantee you is that you won't get shot," Mr. Williams said. So Coach Macci bought a plane ticket and a hotel room, and spent the weekend with the Williams family.

Macci recalls Venus' father showing up at the hotel in a dented Volkswagen bus that had tennis balls, clothes, Coke cans, and about three weeks worth of McDonald's wrappers scattered throughout the wobbly van. "I sat in the passenger seat and there was a spring sticking up. I thought, 'This is amazing.'"

At 7:30 in the morning, Mr. Williams drove him out to East Rancho Dominguez Park, a Compton playground littered with broken glass and beer cans. When Coach Rick Macci first saw Venus that day in California, she was a 10 year-old girl with an "Olive Oyl" body hitting "spaghetti shots" on the battered tennis court. Despite fear for his safety in the ghetto area, Coach Macci started hitting tennis balls with the girls and noticed Venus moved like a newborn colt. He noticed she could cover the court well, but her technique was weak. For example, she hit off her back foot, losing power on her shots and her feet got tangled up more often then not. He also saw Venus' competitive spirit and will. "I thought both of them could be very good but someone has to do a lot of work. For an hour I thought I was pretty much wasting a weekend until the girls took a break," said Macci.

When Venus took a bathroom break, she walked on her hands for about ten feet and started doing flips. Then she did perfect cartwheels for another ten yards. "I'm watching this and the first thing I thought was: 'I've got a female Michael Jordan on my hands,'" recalls coach Macci.

He suddenly became interested. "It jolted me. We started doing competitive drills, one against two. It blew me away. Her footwork improved and her focus was unbelievable. The unforced errors disappeared. She – and Serena – were both so competitive."

Coach Macci instantly became convinced that with the proper training, Venus was a potential champion worth nurturing. He then went back to the Williams home, and Venus' father brought out a video camera and a notepad with 60 questions, largely drawn up from information he had gathered about Macci through the security business he owned. "I've never been interrogated like that before," said Coach Macci. "It scared me, but I respected him because I knew he was so darn serious that whoever he was going to let coach his girls and let into his circle. He wanted to know what he was getting into."

Macci, who now runs an academy in Fort Lauderdale, got the job and the girls entered Rick Macci's International Tennis Academy in 1991. Instead of doing the predictable thing and leaving his daughter's development in the hands of the U.S. Tennis Association and its regional coaches, Williams sold his stake in the family's security services business. He moved the family near Rick Macci's academy. The girls were on scholarship, with Macci's academy providing free tennis lessons, transportation to and from school, and the family with a place to live.

At the academy, coaches stood behind the girls on every shot. They often stopped play to correct mistakes, including practice swings without the ball. The Williams girls did this as much as thirty hours a week. It was almost a full-time job.

In 1993 Venus' parents withdrew her and Serena from Carver Middle School in Delray Beach, Florida and started teaching them at home. As part of their education, they began speaking to inner city school children. "I know I should go back there because that's where I'm from," Venus told *Sports Illustrated*. "It's my roots."

Macci was to coach Venus and Serena for four years in southern Florida, putting in place the beginning of a sophisticated game using her raw talent and athleticism. At the same time, he got to know a patient father and a confident daughter. But still, there were no tournaments.

All the while, Mrs. Williams never feared that her daughters' limited competition and isolated environment would stifle their professional growth. "When we moved to Florida from California, it was to make sure we were doing the right things and teaching the right ways," Oracene said. "Richard has always supervised their workouts and more or less given them instructions on what he wanted to work on. The only thing I worried about was Venus losing her ability to be natural."

From the beginning of the relationship, Richard and Coach Macci had big plans for the girls. "From the day that I met them and started training them, we didn't think juniors," he said. "We talked (Steffi) Graf, (Monica) Seles." (Both Graf and Seles have been highly-ranked women tennis players for the past decade).

Though neither girl played competitively, they did play in exhibition matches where there was less pressure. For example, in October, 1993 Venus traveled to Baltimore and teamed up with 41-year-old former tennis champ Jimmy Connors in a doubles match. Also, she and Serena battled (and beat) baseball star Cal Ripkin and his brother Billy in another match.

Chapter 3:
From Ghetto to Grandstand—
Venus Turns Pro

Venus did not play competitive tennis from 1991 until 1995 because she was busy with school work. The Williams family moved several times within Florida during the four years. Then, in the summer of 1995, the family bought a home on a 10-acre estate with two small lakes in Palm Beach Gardens, Florida. They quickly added three tennis courts.

In the fall of 1994 , against her father's wishes , Venus had decided she was ready to enter the pro orbit. When Venus considered turning professional, the whole family discussed the pros and cons. The girls and their mother voted as a family and the results were 3-2 in favor. Venus' father did not vote. Although he was against it, Richard stood by the decision. "No one in this house," he said, "can make a decision until they get approval from someone else."

Although he had talked her out of playing in the Virginia Slims of Los Angeles tournament two months earlier, this time he was unsuccessful. "Mentally, I don't think my daughter is ready. I don't know any other 14-year-old girl who is ready," he said at the time. He added the WTA's new age-eligibility rules "weren't set up in time to help me."

Coach Macci, who also coached Jennifer Capriati before she turned pro in 1990, thought Venus was ready. "She loves to compete and she wants to compete," he said. "Is she ready? I just know she has ability and she has the potential to be a champion."

"Oakland is a start. It remains to be seen what the finish is," he added. "As long as Venus makes it, that's what people will remember. Anything other than greatness, and she's a failure. That's the tough part."

So, In October of 1995, Venus returned to her native state of California to play in her first professional tennis tournament. By playing at the Bank of the West Classic in Oakland, Venus entered pro tennis two months before new rules designed to keep out 14-year-old girls were to take effect. The Women's Tennis Council, governing body of the WTA Tour, announced a month earlier that beginning in 1995, 14-year-olds would not be allowed to play full tour events. Once they turned 15, they would be limited to just a few tournaments a year. The rule was made because of the self-destructive path Capriati eventually went down after achieving much success at an early age.

"Once the WTA ruling came down, my advice to Richard was to do it because of Venus' ability. He would still be in a position in the future to pick and choose what tournaments to play and how many tournaments to play," said Coach Macci.

But even at 14, Venus had shot up to 6' 1" in height, and was blessed with raw tennis ball-pounding power. Still, there were huge expectations placed on her by fans and the media. It was as if, when it came to Venus, there was as much hype as height. Venus took it all in stride with a great deal of maturity for such a young age.

"I really don't want to be the next hope for women's tennis," she once told the *Palm Beach Post* while taking a break from practice at Rick Macci's tennis academy. "Because I don't want to be a hope for anyone. I have to be a hope for me. I have to go out and play for myself. I don't want to worry about who's watching me or what they're thinking. I have to think about my game."

Venus turned pro in time to leave her options open. According to the new rules, she could play whatever tournaments she wanted to the next year. She said, though, she expected to limit it to three or four, including one in Florida – possibly the Virginia Slims of Florida in Delray Beach.

"I know it won't be a full-time thing," she said. "It will be one week and I'll be able to get away from it."

Immediately, tennis watchers wanted to see if she could duplicate her success in Juniors, or at least deliver what professional tennis needed badly – an athletic young star with charisma and an interesting background. Would she succeed or would it be the Jennifer Capriati story all over again?

Oakland tournament officials fielded more than 200 requests for press credentials to see Venus play her first professional match. Four days earlier they staged a "Meet Venus" day for fans to get her autograph. While there, Venus visited a local high school, an elementary school, and a park. She gave motivational speeches to the students, and easily won them over with her youthful charm.

Despite it being her "coming out" tournament, the grandstands in Oakland, which could seat 10,000 people, were nearly empty. Only about 900 people attended the match, with about one quarter of them from the press. Venus might have been a budding celebrity, but that night she competed with a group of rock legends, the Rolling Stones, who were performing in an adjacent arena.

Though few fans were present, Venus demonstrated that she too was a star. Venus Williams has always been an attention-grabber on the tennis court. Her grace, spirit and self-confidence quickly won fans at Oakland.

From her first tournament, it was evident that Venus was, well, *different*. Unlike many of today's tennis stars who seem just too serious and bland, it's fun watching Venus Williams play tennis. "Venus has something electric that turns on the media, the fans, the common people," her father said. Then there's her hair, or more precisely, her carefully beaded braids. The hard-to-do hair style is a nod to her African-American heritage. The beads bounce and click (and fly off her head!) when she races around the tennis court. A television commentator once described Venus as having "noisy hair." The beads – between 1,800 and 2,000 of them, color-coded to her mood, her outfit or the tournament she's playing in – are as much a part of her as her beautiful tennis serve.

She hits blazing forehands, dazzling backhands and is unbelievably quick. Her long legs propel her to the far corners of the tennis court to get to shots no other player could dream of reaching. The weakest part of her game is her powerful serve. It is faster than any woman's serve. Sometimes, though, she has to ease up to keep it from going long or wide.

Venus overpowered and out-finessed 25-year-old Shaun Stafford 6-3, 6-4 in her professional debut, her hair beads clattering with every stroke In her victory, which earned her $5,350, Venus exhibited a powerful serve, hard ground strokes and a gift for smart shot selection. She frustrated Stafford with drop shots, topspin lobs and on-target passing shots.

"I just got out there and started doing my thing," said Williams, who handled a packed post-match interview with grace and poise. "I was surprised that I wasn't more nervous."

As fans were quickly to learn, when Venus wins a match, there is no look of boredom or overconfidence that

A fifteen-year-old Venus at the Acura Classic in Manhattan Beach, California, August, 1995.

says, "I knew I'd win all along." Nor does she do an obnoxiously loud "in your face" end zone dance like a football player after he scores a touchdown. No, usually when Venus wins, she smiles broadly and does a happy little dance by bending her knees slightly and stretching her hands out in front of her.

Her debut at the start of the tournament at least temporarily silenced critics who charged she was too young for the tennis limelight. But her victory drew a decidedly mixed reaction from her dad. After celebrating the sensational professional debut of his daughter, Richard Williams admitted he was hoping she would lose. Just as when Venus was five years old, he was afraid she'd start to love tennis and her new fame too much.

Her next opponent, in the tournament, the No. 2 player in the world, and reigning French and U.S. Open champion, Arantxa Sanchez Vicario, watched the first set of Williams' match against Stafford. She then slipped out to see the Rolling Stones concert. Before leaving she told a reporter she didn't think Williams was too young to handle the pressure. "I turned professional at 13 myself, so how can I say 14 is too young?" said the 22-year-old Spaniard.

Venus got off to a great start against Sanchez Vicario. She won the first set 6-2 and was leading 3-0 in the second on the strength of a booming serve and powerful groundstrokes. Then fatigue set in and a tired Venus did not win another game in the three-set match. But everyone could see her potential. The question now became, how far, how fast to go?

Despite the loss, Venus cheerfully bounced over to reporters, tilted her head sideways and smiled. When asked about her future plans, Venus said she wasn't sure when she would play again. The tournament in Delray Beach she originally planned to play in was definitely out. Then she surprised everyone when she declared, "I may not play any more tournaments for a while." You see, there was school work to do.

This attitude was one that would continue as Venus' career progressed. Venus says tennis isn't the only thing that's important in her life, surprising for such a budding sensation. Becoming a well-rounded person is important to her. "Things are good and I'm having fun right now," Venus has said. "I'm not playing too much that I get bored of it."

She says the game actually ranks fourth in her life. Ahead of tennis are religion, family and education. You're just as likely seeing Venus wrestle with one of her sisters, or in a book store looking at poetry books, as on a tennis court.

There was no doubt, Venus Williams was going to be one of a kind. She had never looked to any other female tennis players to model herself after. She did have a hero, though. She admits she'd studied tapes of loud and bold John McEnroe, a tennis star of the 1980s as famous for his emotional outbursts as for his considerable skill, because she "liked his attitude." (Although usually composed and respectful when she plays, Venus would display a John McEnroe-type temper at Wimbledon in June of 1998.)

Meanwhile, Venus' father and mother had begun hosting motivational and educational programs for inner-city children. Their overriding message? Education, education, and more education. Tennis was a "game," that would end eventually. An education was forever.

The tremendous emphasis on education was nice, but hard on the heels of Venus' announcement to turn pro came news of a lucrative endorsement deal. Athletic clothing manufacturer Reebok, reportedly offered her 12 million dollars. Fans may speculate why a high school or college diploma is necessary as a fallback. (Serena would eventually sign a deal with athletic shoe maker, Puma).

Richard has said there are other endorsements, but that he has also turned down many, many more than they've accepted. Mr. Williams said he rejected most offers from management companies and companies wanting Venus to endorse their products. He said once if she did, there would be pressure on her to play more. "I want her to play for Venus and her dogs. I don't want her to perform for anybody."

Over the years, Venus' parents have been accused of exploiting their daughters merely to make lots of money. They vehemently deny that they have done that. Venus' mother once said that just the thought of living off her children makes her ill. Likewise, Venus' father has said, "I've been broke all my life, and Venus doesn't want to be poor … I'd rather have a healthy daughter than a million dollars."

In the meantime, Serena had slowly been learning more about her sport. Serena, who according to her family is both a perfectionist and has greater actual potential as a tennis player than Venus, was set to play her first pro match. When, just like Venus, Serena turned pro at 14-years-old, she made her WTA Tour debut in the qualifying round of a small Canadian tournament in 1995. She played well, but did not win. The event scarcely received mention in the press, unlike the hoopla when Venus turned pro a year earlier. The lack of attention didn't bother Serena; she took it in stride.

Serena would not play in another tournament through 1996. Richard wanted her to concentrate on school work, and though she wanted to match herself against pro competitions, Serena, as usual, obeyed her father.

Chapter 4:
Learning Their Craft

Venus Williams didn't play in another tennis tournament until August, 1995. Her final preparations for the the Acura Classic in Los Angeles consisted of several days of vacation in California with her family. In the tournament, Venus lost badly in her first round match to a relatively unknown player, Asa Carlsson, 6-4, 6-1.

No matter which way Venus turned, there were people criticizing her and her parents. Some attacked them for allowing Venus to turn pro at 14.

"I think it's moronic," said Mary Carillo, a tennis commentator for CBS and ESPN. "I am disappointed Richard allowed Venus to succumb to the pressure of big time tennis. There are so many girls like Tracy Austin and Monica Seles who don't even finish high school."

On the other hand, because she played a limited schedule of tournaments, there were those who slammed them for not doing more. At the Acura Classic, sports writers said she had "an erratic service toss," and could only hit the ball down the middle of the court. But she was also described as looking spectacular with her beaded braids and white silk vest with a bow in the back, an outfit her mother sewed herself.

Venus only played in two more tournaments in 1995, including a return trip in October to the Bank of the West Classic in Oakland. Her biggest career win to that date occurred in Oakland, over highly-ranked Amy Frazier. Venus beat Frazier, in three sets in the second round. By the end of 1995 she was ranked 205th on the women's tour, barely a blip on the tennis radar screen, though her potential was enormous.

One measure of just how highly the tennis world regarded Venus, or at least her potential as a player, came early in 1995 when Venus was named to the U.S. Fed Cup squad by tennis legend, Billie Jean King. The Fed Cup is a prestigious tournament where players from one country team up against players from other countries. "I selected her because of her potential," King said . "The family understands she has to play (in pro tournaments) and prove herself. But it's a long-term issue."

When Serena turned pro in 1995, her former coach Rick Macci said, "In six months, she'll be ready to rumble." Regardless, her father was determined to have her follow pretty much the same schedule as her sister's.

Serena would have a harder time abiding by her father's rules. She wanted to play in more tournaments than her older sister was allowed to. "I don't think I want to stay out [of tennis] as much as Venus did," said Serena. "Not to say it was wrong, but I think what she did was a good thing for her."

Richard Williams won out. Limited to one tournament that first year, Serena didn't play at all in 1996.

Coach Rick Macci made a new move. Named director of tennis at Fort Lauderdale's Inverrary resort, Coach Macci had to drive back and forth between the resort and the Williams house. Soon after, the Williams-Macci alliance crumbled. After coach Macci had worked with Venus and Serena for four years, the partnership broke up over differences about training and the limited professional tournament schedule Mr. Williams favored. Macci thought Venus needed to start playing Junior tournaments and get some match experience.

The Williams girls then tried another tennis camp, Nick Bollettieri's academy, but the Williams family lasted only six weeks there. Venus' parents took them out and said they were through with tennis academies. "I thought they looked at them as a commodity, and you know what happens when a commodity gets used up," said Richard. "They throw one away and get another one."

Once again, Richard Williams said he was more interested in building healthy people than tennis legends, preferring at-home hitting partners and hours of practice to tournament travel. Since then, Richard and Oracene Williams have been their daughters' coaches.

Looking back, Coach Macci might not agree with how Richard Williams handled every detail of his daughter's tennis career, and he's had a few disagreements of his own with him. But Macci respects the way Richard has been able to educate Venus. "All I know is he has a well-rounded daughter and she's incredibly nice," he said. "I think that was more important to him."

Even today, much is made of Richard's lack of tennis knowledge. As Coach Macci points out, Venus didn't go straight from the ghetto to great tennis. Much coaching and effort was required. "Six hours a day, six days a week for four years," says Macci of Venus' practice schedule under his tutelage. "There wasn't a day that the girl wouldn't hit 200 serves."

Over the last several years, Venus and Serena have practiced only with each other or with hard-hitting male tennis partners. In addition, they have learned Tae Kwon Do, worked out with a professional boxer, practiced gymnastic moves, and even thrown a football around in as a part of their training They have even used a hula hoop to work on lower-body coordination. The girls' training led to a greater appreciation of their talents among tennis experts.

In 1996, Venus' schedule picked up a little bit. She played in five tournaments, but won none. Her greatest success that year took place at the Acura Classic when she advanced to the third round before losing to the eventual winner, Steffi Graf.

But that wasn't the most notable event at the tournament. At 32 years of age, Zina Garisson Jackson, the most successful African-American woman of her generation, with fourteen Corel WTA Tour titles to her name, was the oldest player in the tournament. Venus Williams, now 16 years-old, was the youngest. Only time would tell if the 1996 Acura represented the passing of the African-American women's tennis torch.

One other important event happened on the Women's tour that year, foreshadowing things to come. At the Bausch & Lomb Championships, Venus smacked a 108 miles-per-hour serve. It was the ninth-fastest serve on the tour that year.

Venus continued to avoid playing in most tournaments. She still practiced a lot, but only with Serena and male hitting partners. Tennis observers said "we told you so!" when she struggled through her limited tournament schedule. She seemed destined to end her second year on the tour as little more than someone's opponent.

Her lack of success didn't phase her father one bit. In fact, he said he was paying Venus $50 for every match she lost, trying to encourage her to quit. Once again, Richard was doing and saying the unexpected. "For me," he said, "It's almost immaterial whether she wins or loses." In fact, he wished both girls would quit playing tennis. "It's not important anymore for them to be good players. It used to be. No more. What I want is for them to be good human beings."

At the end of 1996, Venus was ranked 211th. She was going backwards, actually moving down in the rankings. However, her popularity was going straight up.

Because Venus rose from a Los Angeles ghetto to the professional tennis circuit by working hard and following a plan, she had been in great demand to speak to other teens who faced similar problems. In 1995, Venus was honored for her charitable work by the Sports Image Foundation; the award was for conducting tennis clinics in low-income areas.

One organization that called on her for help was the Urban League. In September, 1996, Venus, along with Ms. Thyra Echols-Starr, director of the Palm Beach County Urban League, spoke to about 250 kids, parents and teachers at the Belle Glade Elementary school. At the back-to-school hot dog social they told the kids about the Urban League's new program, Doing the Right Thing.

The program teams up about fifty middle and high school students from Palm Beach County as mentors including Venus, and her sister Serena. They meet with 120 fourth and fifth-graders at area schools to keep them focused on learning and seeing that there is more to life than poverty. Some have never been to a beach, some have never been to a theater or to a mall.

Each month, the mentors and students meet to

Serena in a losing effort against Lindsay Davenport at the Ameritech Cup in Chicago, November 1997.

encourage better grades, higher attendance and volunteer activities, such as visiting nursing homes. "Hopefully, it will have an impact on them – that I didn't come from the best neighborhood in the world and they will have to work hard in life," Venus told the *Palm Beach Post.* "Education is the most important thing."

But Venus was still best-known for her tennis. Early in 1997, Venus played three tournaments. In March, she registered her first win over a top 10 player (Iva Majoli) in the third round at the Evert Cup in Indian Wells, California. In the match, Venus had one serve that registered 109-miles-per-hour on the radar gun.

In the quarter-finals she lost to eventual champion Lindsay Davenport, the eighth-ranked player in the world. The match was decided by a third-set tie-breaker. Davenport had a tougher time than she expected against Venus. "She's going to be one of the great stars of the future, maybe this year. I was lucky to get the win," Davenport said. Venus' ranking soared to 114th after the tournament.

Although pleased with her play at Indian Wells, Venus was homesick. She missed her dogs; she missed her car; and now that she was no longer studying at home, she missed her school. Her father said as long as she maintained an "A" average, he would let her play in more tournaments.

Venus' grades did remain high, and she entered the Lipton Championships. Again, she produced an upset by winning against Jennifer Capriati. She lost to the eventual champion, Martina Hingis, in straight sets. Afterwards, Hingis was ranked number one. Despite her loss, Venus boldly predicted that she and Serena would soon be battling for the number one ranking. Reporters scurried for their notepads, and Venus was labeled a braggart.

Also in 1997, Richard allowed Venus to make her Grand Slam debut at the French Open in May. There are four Grand Slam tournaments each year; The Australian Open, the French Open, Wimbledon in England, and the U.S. Open in New York. They are the premier tennis tournaments for both women and men. The Lipton Championships are considered by many to rank just below the Grand Slam events.

Before Venus was allowed to go to France, Mr. Williams made her study French. She had to master a basic vocabulary before he would give his okay. Venus traveled to France with her mother and Serena. Richard stayed at home, saying he didn't like to fly.

The French Open marked Venus' first competition away from the U.S. Her first round opponent, Naoko Sawamatsu of Japan, was ranked a more impressive No. 45 in the world. The slipping and sliding on the clay surface of the Roland Garros court at first hindered the play of the tall and lanky Venus. She quickly adjusted.

Towards the end of the marathon encounter, Venus was finally serving for the match at 5-4 in the third set. But she fell apart in the 10th game, double-faulting twice before losing her serve on a third break point for Sawamatsu. She finally pulled it out on a third match point in the 12th game when a frustrated Sawamatsu smacked a backhand wide.

Ultimately, her grit and determination delivered a

hard fought 6-2, 6-7 (2-7), 7-5 first round victory in a long two hours, 39 minutes. Afterwards, Venus said almost nonchalantly, "I played a lot better than I thought I would."

Despite only being 16, and lacking professional experience, Venus spoke to the press afterwards like a long-term veteran of the women's tour. " I think in a lot of ways it's like any other tournament – you still have to play your match, you still sweat, still run."

But not every game came easily to Venus. Her next match against Nathalie Tauziat of France didn't go as well. Wearing a unique silvery bodysuit, she lost.

Venus next traveled to England in June. In the Direct Line Insurance Championships in Eastbourne, Venus beat highly ranked Chandra Rubin (a fellow African-American) in the first round. In the second round she faced Nathalie Tauziat again, and again, she lost.

Venus was planning something special for her second Grand Slam tournament appearance, the Wimbledon tournament in June, 1997. Though she wore white beads in her hair during her French Open debut and blue and red in previous tournaments that year, she said she was leaning toward a system of color-coding according to where she's playing. Williams said she was thinking about different beads For Wimbledon, where the official colors are green and purple. "I am seeing green, purple," she told reporters. "What do you think? I'm contemplating."

Venus entered Wimbledon ranked 59th in the world. The press clamored for information on this unique American tennis player. With Serena at her side, Venus fielded questions like a veteran. When asked how she planned to celebrate her 17th birthday, she said that Jehovah's Witnesses didn't celebrate birthdays. Asked if she admired any other players, she answered, "No, I don't." Asked if she could be the savior of U.S. tennis she said, "Yes, I think so." With answers like that, Venus wasn't making any friends on the Women's Tour.

It rained for five days at Wimbledon, postponing the matches. The more veteran players complained about boredom. But not Venus. She spent her time sightseeing with her sister and mother.

She visited what is considered the No. 1 tourist attraction in the city : The Tower Of London, where the Royal Jewels are housed. Williams joked that "I won't tell you my plans now," when asked if she saw anything she'd like to take home.

During the rain delay at the All England Club at Wimbledon, a small controversy erupted about how it would be handled if any of the 17-year-old American's beads fell out during play. Williams revealed what she was told about the potential bead-flying problem in a press conference held during a dreary and drenched Friday at Wimbledon.

"It all started, I looked in the paper and it said, 'Venus has been warned,' and that never happened," Williams said. "So I asked an official at the WTA and she just told me that they would just play the "let" rule for the first few times. After that, it would then be a point (penalty)."

Venus thought the ruling was unfair. "If a bead flies off, no one is going to be looking at my hair. The opponent – if they were looking at my hair, there would be a problem, they wouldn't be interested in playing tennis. And if a bead flies off, it's so small, you're not really going to notice it. Then, you know, the umpire might tell the ball boy to pick it up. It's not even a disturbance."

The crowd at Wimbledon loved the new purple and green beads adorning her hair. In response to the huge fan demand to see her, tournament officials scheduled her first round game on one of the feature courts. These courts are usually reserved for only the top players and matches.

During Venus' first match against Magdalena Grzybowska of Poland, Serena sat in the stands reading *A Tale of Two Cities*, her face covered by a screen of white beads.

Obviously the beads didn't hinder Ms. Grzybowska. She won, nailing backhand shot after backhand shot for winners and eliminating Venus from the tournament. Afterwards, Grzybowska said she thought Venus was a huge talent but was surprised at her strategy during the match. Especially giving her the opportunity to use her backhand. "My backhand is my best shot," she pointed out.

Then Serena was asked for her opinion. She showed a quick sense of humor by quipping, "I've read *Great Expectations*, but I like this one better," she said, tapping the book cover.

Serena was having plenty of off-court time to root for his sister. In 1997 she would participate in only a handful of tournaments, but still would see her ranking begin to climb. At the Ameritech Cup in Chicago, she knocked off both Monica Seles and Mary Pierce, two players who were ranked in the top ten. This was a considerable feat. She then twisted her ankle and lost her quarter-final match. Afterwards she told reporters, "I think I've emerged." And indeed she had. Soon after the tournament, her ranking rose from 304th to 100th, quite a jump for the budding star.

After Wimbledon, Venus' next tournament was the Toshiba Tennis Classic in San Diego. During three qualifying rounds – unseeded players have to qualify for the actual tournament – and in her first round match she didn't lose a set. She then lost to Martina Hingis, again.

Soon after, Venus played in two more tournaments. In Los Angeles' Acura Classic she made it to the second round before losing to Anke Huber. In the du Maaurier Open held in Toronto, Canada, she was knocked out in the first round by Nathalie Dechy.

Though tennis fans were starting to warm up to Venus, some experts thought it would be just a matter of time before she would become yesterday's news, tomorrow's great "has been." She just didn't seem capable of adjusting to her opponent or of recovering when things went wrong.

"Venus has been kept out of so many tournaments she doesn't have a competitive foundation," said Kevin O'Connor of the Saddlebrook Academy. "She has one more year of an aura of excitement about her before she becomes an old song."

This period indeed was difficult for Venus. She had so much potential, and had not yet proved it on the court. There were other difficulties. Being named after a mythological goddess isn't all its cracked up to be. "To tell you the truth, my name is almost a curse," revealed Venus later in her career. "Every time I go on the phone, they say, 'What's your name? I say, Venus. What Zenus. Venus. What Zenus? No, Venus.' Every day people send me mail saying Zenus. It's very discouraging."

On the "Tonight Show Starring Jay Leno," Venus revealed she was still having problems with her name. "The women at the driver's license bureau just couldn't get it right," she said. I'm thinking of changing it to Venus. Just Venus. But my mother thinks my middle names, Ebone Starr, are too pretty to drop."

Another thing that irks Williams is when people who

recognize her start serenading her with Frankie Avalon's "Venus," a tune she doesn't care for because "it's old."

"The worst thing is that, when people come up to me and start singing like that song, and popping their fingers and things," Venus told *Tennis* magazine.

The training of the young star takes most of her day. Tennis can be a grueling sport, with matches lasting two hours or more. According to *Tennis* magazine, here's how Venus Williams stays in shape:

Three times a week, Williams hits the weight room at 6 a.m. for 75 minutes of arm, shoulder and triceps exercises. "I want to make sure I don't have any injuries and that I maintain my muscle weight," she says. She also jumps rope intensely for five minutes to warm up before practicing.

Sometimes she goes to an aerobics class to improve her footwork. "Besides it's fun to try to keep up with the newest steps," Williams says.

Much of her workout consists of drills her father and coach, Richard, borrowed from other sports. She throws a football or baseball the length of a court for 30 minutes to help her service motion. Also, she and Serena play soccer on the court for 30 minutes to help with footwork.

To fine-tune her reflexes for volleys, Venus works out with boxing gloves and a speed bag. To improve her balance, she surfs. For stamina she'll run a mile and do wind sprints. "I want to enhance all of my game," she says. "Things like treadmills and StairMasters bore me. I don't even own a bike. I like being outside."

This doesn't mean that all Venus does for fun has to do with tennis, tennis and more tennis. Venus hates when people ask her to describe a typical day in her life. "It's like the wind blowing," she explains with a shrug. "It can change direction."

But the one thing that does not change from day to day is the family's faith in God. It's part of the foundation the Williams parents laid for their children. Both Venus and Serena are devoted Jehovah's Witnesses, and attend religious meetings three times a week. Throughout their lives, the sisters have witnessed to strangers by telling them about God, although Venus notes that it is becoming impractical. "Getting more popular, I don't know if I can go house to house anymore," she said. "People are going to say, 'What about the tennis?' I'll say, 'What about this?'"

The religious faith of the girls was to be an important part of life as their careers progressed. Later, during an interview at the U.S. Open tournament, Venus was asked how she handled the pressure. She responded, "I just remember tennis isn't the most important thing that's happening in my life. A lot of times it can get larger than life. If it gets too important, it becomes more of a job and a chore."

When asked what the most important thing in her life was, Venus looked directly at the questioner and said, "serving God is." And she once told *Tennis* magazine; "I think that some of the reasons why a lot of people say Serena and I were good kids – we're obedient, never go crazy – is because of our beliefs ... In the Bible it tells us that disobedient children do not live all their days. I believe that.

"We believe it's just like tennis, you can't just go once a month and expect your game to be on top," Venus said of her family's dedication to religion. "We believe in good association with fellow Witnesses, not becoming too involved with people that don't have the same beliefs and same values that we do."

Richard Williams says their faith and schooling are more a part of their being than tennis. "The most interesting thing about my daughters," Richard said, "is they love God, they love their family, themselves, their education. I see a lot of stories, but people don't write about how educated they are, how polite they are."

The Williams' emphasis on God and education is apparent. Both girls are bright and articulate. "Education is more important than tennis right now," Venus told *Seventeen* magazine in April, 1996. "Whatever I put in my head will stay there and that's not necessarily true of tennis." Back then Venus' favorite subject was science. "Can you believe that in 1923 explorers found a prehistoric fish off the coast of Madagascar that was supposed to be extinct, like five hundred million years ago? Learning about that stuff is so cool."

Besides religion and education, family also comes

before tennis. "My parents were taught that family should be together, and that's how they taught us," Venus says. "I definitely don't plan to move away from my family. I'll probably live on the next lot."

Is there anything that bugs her about her family? Sure, when her father beats her at Galaga, the video game. "Right now, my goal is to become better than my dad," Williams said admitting she was about 4,000 points behind.

Once when she was asked about criticism that she is aloof from other players on tour, she shrugged. "I'm looking to win matches, to be the best. I'm not looking for friends. You really can't find a friend these days. You have your family, you have your God, and that's about it."

But this doesn't mean Venus does *everything* her parents want. For instance, there's a few chores she tries to avoid. "I'm not a worker," Venus said. "I found out that when I do things like fold clothes and wash dishes, my back starts hurting. I'm not kidding. Like, when I lie down, there are pains. I found that I can't do those things."

Chapter 5:
First Success

Before the U.S. Open in September 1997, Venus had yet to reach a tournament final. Her overall record of ten wins and nine losses was hardly the record of a legend in the making. Still, because of her sudden increase in tournament play and modest success, her ranking climbed to 66th in the world.

New York, the media capital of the world, can be a cruel and unforgiving place. Then again, if someone captures the imagination of the local fans, they will be embraced, lifted high on their shoulders. New York fans particularly like someone different, someone unique. If they're good at what they do, all the better.

African-American tennis legend Arthur Ashe was that kind of person. The 1997 U.S. Open was held in the National Tennis Center's pristine 23,000-seat Arthur Ashe Stadium. The Center is in Flushing Meadow, Queens, a borough, or county adjoining Manhattan.

Once again, Richard Williams stayed away. He told *Sports Illustrated* he stayed in Florida rather than go to the Open and "sit there moving my head left and right, screaming and cheering and looking silly."

Williams admitted talking to a psychiatrist who told him if he wanted his daughter to be successful, to "try your best not to be there when she plays." Trying not to offend her father, Venus reluctantly agreed it was good advice. "I would prefer to think for myself," she said.

Williams said he would probably talk to Venus once or twice before the match and that he sent her off with written instructions. He doubted he'd do any more coaching until she came home. "I don't want her to say, 'Dad was trying to coach me from a thousand miles away,' he said. "I want her to say, 'I'm so proud you're my dad.'" Instead he promised to stay in close contact with Oracene via cell phone.

It was a tournament perfectly designed for Venus Williams. Not only was the tournament being played in a new facility named for an African-American, it also began on Althea Gibson's 70th birthday. Ms. Gibson is the most famous African-American woman tennis player of all time.

Everything was in place for Venus to make a big splash on the tennis scene. However, her game needed improvement. Although her athleticism and power were obvious, at times she looked almost lost on the court. At Wimbledon she had served with a broken racket string in her first-round loss. Broken strings can cause a loss of power and control of one's shots. It's a major blunder tennis players seldom make.

By the time the Open began, tennis experts were mumbling that Venus needed a *real* tennis coach, badly, and was probably too proud to admit it. They also "tsk, tsked" that her "coaching" father chose not to come at all.

As far as the press and tennis experts were concerned, Venus was quickly becoming yesterday's phenomenon. Reporters were saying the youngster most likely to make a splash at the Open was either 16-year-old Anna Kournikova of Russia, who made it to the Wimbledon semi-finals, or 15-year-old Mirjana Lucic of Croatia. Martina Hingis claimed Lucic was "even better than Kournikova and Williams."

Then something strange happened. Kournikova won one match and then lost. Lucic won two matches and then lost. Meanwhile, Venus Williams won two matches against Larisa Neiland and Gala Leon Garcia, and seemed to be improving each time. "It used to be that I didn't fully understand that I didn't have to go for winners every time," she said. "I never took too much pace off the ball. It wasn't part of my game." So just like that, she practiced hitting slower shots to exact spots loaded with spin.

For example, she slowed her 110-mph serve to 90-100 mph against Sandrine Testud in the quarter-finals. She had noticed her opponent was having more trouble with the ball's spin than with speed. "I didn't feel as much pressure to hit great shots, hit them on the lines" Williams reasoned. "Sometimes just deep, well-placed [shots] puts pressure on my opponent to do something better, and that is the game I really hadn't played before." She said she "borrowed" the new various-speeds approach from her younger sister, Serena.

Many players need months before they use new tactics they have been practicing every day for weeks. Venus made the adjustment in the middle of a match. "I've been able to understand more, quicker than a lot of people. "It didn't seem extremely dramatic," she said.

That shift in her game plan, plus her lifelong reputation, gave Williams an aura usually reserved for only the top players. "We create it in our own heads: We're playing Venus!" said Joannette Kruger after losing to Williams, 6-2, 6-3 in the fourth round. "Yes, it's crazy. I don't know what to think of it."

At 23, Kruger remembers when she was 17 years old admiring all the top players and saying, "Wow," when she played them. "Here's Venus at 17 and thinking she's this wonderful, great player. I don't know where you get it, but she has it," said Ms. Kruger.

Kruger said she was intimidated before she even walked onto the U.S. Open's stadium court for the first time, which already had her nervous enough. She called it crazy that such a young player gave her the jitters, even though Venus had a reputation as a top upcoming member of the tour. "I think she handled the situation much better than I did," Kruger said.

During the changeover Venus suddenly grinned at her. "It came over as, 'Do you have anything else to show me?'" Kruger said. Venus later said it was an amused look, not a smile. Kruger was the second player in two matches to say she got so angry she beat herself instead of forcing Williams to beat her. Eighth-seed Anke Huber, who lost to Venus two days earlier, was the first.

Venus was quickly developing a new reputation, as brash and arrogant. Venus hadn't made many friends on the tour, perhaps because her sister and mother were always with her. Some players figured she probably didn't need the same sort of companionship that players traveling alone might need.

Suddenly, it seemed every woman player had a "here's how Venus snubbed me," story. Every step she took toward a dream finals showdown against the World Number One player, Martina Hingis, seemed to unearth more resentment of Williams and her family. Players complained publicly about her arrogance, her unfriendly demeanor, her trash-talking.

Lindsay Davenport said when she ran into Venus on the grounds at the Evert Cup in March, she said hello, to her face, and Venus didn't respond. "I learned not to do that again," she concluded.

Some players wondered if it might be an intimidation ploy. Regardless, Davenport thought it motivated her to win the Indian Wells quarter-final.

Venus is surprised when people put down her attitude.

She says she has been taught to play to win. "Why don't you guys tell me what they want me to do?" she said to reporters after hearing Kruger's comment. "They should come up to me and say, 'Venus, I want you to smile so I can feel better.'

"When I want to smile, I'll smile. If I don't want to, I'm not going to. I think it's a little bit peevish. Smiling, what does that have to do with anything?"

In women's tennis, everything. Young players are expected to respect the more experienced players. Once you've made it big you can say or do practically anything you want. Martina Hingis can make cocky statements all day long and no one minds, because she's Number One and says it with a grin.

Could the resentment be racially motivated? Asked if the tension surrounding Williams had to do with race, Davenport said, "I don't feel it's a problem of race. I feel like she's separated herself from us for whatever reason. The players in the locker room love Chanda Rubin, and Zina Garrison is a good friend. Some people have tried, but you can only try so much."

Perhaps the truth of the matter was, Venus was quickly becoming (again) the biggest story in women's tennis, a sport literally dying for lack of a star. And it seemed as if the other players hated her for it. One high-level tennis official who had been inside the women's locker room throughout the tournament, said,

"The women are appalling. They have been nasty and mean to Venus."

But Venus was hardly guilt-free. She was, and is, stand-offish and works to keep herself isolated inside her family. Also, her voluble self-confidence often grates on some people. Players frequently have said they resented Venus' refusal to give credit to her opponents after a match.

Her situation was similar to what had happened to Tiger Woods in golf, a young player who had turned pro amid tremendous media hoopla. It was only after winning the Masters tournament, and securing a place as a top money-winner, that his true merits began to be appreciated. Golf legend Jack Nicklaus once was asked by the *San Francisco Examiner* if other players were envious of Tiger Woods. He replied, "If you don't think the guys on the tour are jealous of him, you've got another think coming. They're jealous as can be. They're going to have to raise their game a notch. If they don't, they're going to be playing for second every week." Was the same thing happening with Venus and her competitors?

Even though the tennis players found fault with Venus, the fans loved her. They loved her not just for winning, but for handing out beads from her hair after matches. They loved her for leaping up against a wall alongside the court to reach and kiss her mother. They loved her for being different. They loved her for being Venus Ebone Starr Williams.

Meanwhile, Serena was watching her sister become a controversial star. She naturally yearned to be more like her older sibling.

The world had heard less about Serena. Her identity, off and on the tennis court revolved around Venus. Venus had beaded her hair first. Serena copied it. The two girls were different, though. Venus had been called arrogant and aloof. Serena was more outgoing, even charming.

Venus says Serena is a "kind of perfectionist." Early in her professional career, Serena admitted that she wanted to "win every point," the same type of attitude that fueled the drive of John McEnroe, who is her role model as well as that of Venus.

Oracene Williams once shared some differences she saw between her two tennis star daughters. "With Venus, everything come so easy," she said. "It's just a natural ability, no matter what it is, athletic or academic. With Serena, it comes a little bit harder, but it makes her work harder, too. She's more of a stick-to-it person."

They even have a different style in tennis. Serena, says her father, benefitted from such practice partners as John McEnroe and Pete Sampras. "Because Serena couldn't beat those guys with power, she had to learn to do angles and drop shots," Richard Williams said. "Right now I think Serena is hitting angles and drop shots better than anyone."

Venus, too, had much to prove on the court, and just at that moment, in the Open. Two days after defeating Sandrine Testud in the quarter-finals, Venus came into Arthur Ashe Stadium for her sixth match of her first U.S. Open. When she did, she became the first black woman in the semi-finals since Zina Garrison Jackson in 1989, and the first unseeded semi-finalist since Yugoslavia's Mima Jausovec in 1976. She was also one of three players making their Grand Slam semi-final debut, joining her opponent, 11th seed Irina Spirlea, and sixth seed Lindsay Davenport.

If Venus won the semi-final, she would become the first unseeded woman to reach a U.S. Open final. Any of the four semi-finalists who won this tournament would be a first-time winner. It also would be the first time Steffi Graf, Monica Seles or Arantxa Sanchez Vicario hadn't taken the title since 1990, when Gabriela Sabatini won. And although Spirlea had been this tournament's hot player, knocking off two top-five players in Amanda Coetzer and Monica Seles, experts didn't put reaching the final out of Venus' reach.

Few doubted her confidence. Whether she could handle Spirlea's serve, strong forehand and court quickness was the bigger question. Tennis experts said if Venus continued to mix up her shots more, she just might win. That was Venus' plan. "I realize I have to mix it up, take some pace off, lift it over," she said. However, Spirlea was expected to adjust to Venus' strategy changes much better than her previous opponents.

Up until this point, everything was going right for Venus. She was winning and becoming a favorite of both the media and the fans. Then it happened: the incident; the bump. As a result, Venus got a taste of the other side of New York media attention.

After the seventh game of the second set Venus and Irina Spirlea collided. They bumped torsos at the net post on a changeover as they crossed the court to get to their seats. Venus wore an intense expression as she bounced quickly toward her chair, and Spirlea had a sour, angry look as she came from the other direction more slowly.

"I was thinking about going home," she remarked later, "and I said, 'That's not the right thing to think, Venus, you've got to hold strong. Push those thoughts out of the way. It's not over. She has to win a point to win the match.' She had two match points. Somehow, she didn't win them. Somehow, I didn't let her win them."

The match continued, with Venus dismissing the incident and playing with confidence. She drilled a perfect running backhand that zipped by Spirlea and left the Romanian stunned. Williams then fended off another break when Spirlea's forehand shot went into the net. Two points later, with Spirlea serving, Williams lunged to whack a forehand return into the corner, and Spirlea could only dump it into the net to set up match point for Venus. The crowd in the packed arena roared their approval.

When Spirlea, who had knocked out former champion Monica Seles, sailed a backhand wide to lose the final point, Venus leaped in the air and bounced up and down in disbelief. Afterwards Venus said, "There's a lot of myths floating around. A lot of people believe you have to be match tough, and I do agree that you have to play a little bit. I look back on a year ago and I didn't know what to do. But it hasn't taken me long to learn, hasn't taken me many matches. So maybe a fraction of the talk about me will stop."

The championship her parents always told her she would one day win was now within her reach. However, Venus had never beaten or even come to close to beating her next opponent, Martina Hingis. Before she could face Martina, however, she had to face a controversy; the bumping incident with Spirlea.

After she lost, Spirlea took the collision personally, saying she was tired of detouring out of Venus' path. "I've done it all the time. I turn, but she just walks," Spirlea told the press. "I was not going to move, and she never tried to turn. I wanted to see if she would turn, and she didn't." The media accused Spirlea of cursing to describe Venus who in reality, not only bumped into her during the match but also bumped her out of contention. Spirlea had taken verbal swipes at several popular teens in the tournament in the past week, but this was different. This was about Venus Williams.

At first, Venus' jaw dropped after hearing Spirlea's

statement from the post-match news conference. She recovered in a moment, saying she couldn't change what others though about her. She also shrugged off the confrontation. Noting that neither player was injured from the bump, she added, "I thought we both weren't looking. I'm sorry she feels that way. It's not a big thing to me. No one said, 'Excuse me.'" The media, smelling a story, looked for evidence that the bump was as a racial incident.

It's hard to talk about Venus Williams and not bring up the topic of race. She is only one of very few African-American women to play the sport professionally.

Even Venus' parents fanned the flames of controversy. "I think they're afraid of her," Oracene told the *New York Daily News*. "They want her to be their Stepin' Fetchit." (the actor Stepin' Fetchit was a black stereotype from decades ago.)

Richard Williams, who will not back down from anybody when it comes to his daughters, told an Associated Press reporter by phone, "There have been a lot of people taking cheap shots at Venus. I've heard sly remarks.

"I think what happened to Venus was a racial thing," he added. "I've seen a lot of racial things happen to my baby." Richard then made matters worse. He said he and Venus had both heard players use the word "n-word." He said Spirlea's bump was racially motivated and called Spirlea "a big, ugly, tall, white turkey."

Fortunately, the finals needed to be played and, at least for a while, everyone focused on the Williams-Hingis showdown. Martina Hingis said she wasn't worried, even after Venus' fabulous performances in previous matches. "Venus is just a player who has nothing to lose," said Hingis. "The best feeling you can have out there is knowing no one is better than you. Even though she also thinks she can beat everyone in the world, I'll love to see later on who is going to be the better one."

Richard Williams countered by saying Venus had spoken to Althea Gibson. "Venus spoke to Althea this morning. She's very proud of Venus. Althea is very uplifted right now."

The press had fun comparing Venus and Ms. Gibson. They were alike as players: tall, athletic, graceful and black. Gibson made three straight U.S. Open finals in the late '50s, winning two, and broke a social barrier. Venus planned on becoming the first black woman since Gibson to raise the trophy.

Venus became the first unseeded woman finalist in the Open era and the first to go so far in her debut since Pam Shriver in 1978. No final in Grand Slam history has featured two players as young as the 17-year-old Williams and the 16-year-old Hingis (who eliminated Lindsay Davenport in their semi-final match). Their meeting, the experts said, could well be the beginning of a popular rivalry for years to come.

Rick Macci thought Venus would have her hands full with Martina. "Mentally, Hingis is well beyond her years," Macci said. "But if she can get into Hingis' head and she gets a little tight, Venus can beat her."

It was not to be. In the finals, Martina Hingis hammered Venus (who had quickly jumped all the way from 66th to 27th in the rankings with her showing at Flushing Meadow) 6-0, 6-4 in the final. It was Hingis' third Grand Slam victory of the year; she had previously won the Australian Open and Wimbledon. Her U.S. Open victory also pushed her record against Venus to 3-0.

Though the match was filled with tension at the beginning, Martina managed to add a little fun. During a changeover she raced to her seat to avoid a collision with Venus. "I saw her previous match," she said with a smile. "I wanted to make sure I was faster than her."

Despite the loss, Venus' progress as a player was undeniable; almost overnight she had become a force every player — but one — feared. "She got better and better," said Hingis after their match. "For the first time she showed that she can play great. I didn't know she could play that well."

For Venus, it was a huge payday. She earned $350,000 just for making the Open finals. She had begun 1997 with a 10-9 record, only $31,000 in career earnings, and a ranking of 204th. For 1997, up to the U.S. Open, she was 27-9 over all and 7-2 in Grand Slam matches.

Unfortunately, just after Venus' appearance in the final, her press conference deteriorated into a standoff between her and white reporters repeatedly and vainly trying to elicit a response to her father's earlier remarks about Spirlea and "the bump." As words flew, and one black reporter walked out in protest of his colleagues' questions, Venus seemed to shrink in her chair.

However, she remained poised and seemed to be the only one showing maturity way beyond her 17 years. "I think with this moment in the first year in Arthur Ashe Stadium, it all represents everyone being together, everyone having a chance to play," she said. "So I think this is definitely ruining the mood, these questions about racism."

It was like nothing tennis had ever seen. "It was a little mess," said Hingis of the charged atmosphere. "Like a boxing fight at the end."

Does Venus feel she needs to carry the burden of being a racial representative? "If I'd lived prior to the 1980s, it would have been different, because I would have been playing to prove African Americans are equal. Now, I don't necessarily feel I have to play for black people, because obviously they're doing everything in all sports. If I can go out there and play for myself and not feel I have to stand for something other than what I want to do, that's good."

Zina Garrison, who played on the women's tour for 15 years, knows the pressures Williams faces. "She's in a great position, and she's been raised to be in that position as an African-American in a mostly white sport," said Garrison, who works with inner-city junior tennis players in Houston. "It helps her that she has the strength, confidence and arrogance you need to become the top player in the world."

The shame, of course, lies in the bitter fact that Williams's Open debut will be remembered as a mixed blessing for the game. If both players were of a the same race, the incident would have been soon forgotten. People are left to wonder, though, what the ghost of the always-dignified Arthur Ashe would make of the whole affair.

Following her strong showing in the U.S. Open, Venus Williams got lazy. She was unable to follow through, losing in the opening round of her next tournament, at the Porshe Grand Prix in Filderstadt, Germany. She then lost in the quarter-finals to Lindsay Davenport at the European Indoor Championships. She also lost in the quarter-finals of the Ladies Kremlin Cup to Jana Novotna.

"It wasn't that easy because I had to go overseas to play," Williams said. "And I guess I really didn't practice that much. I got lazy; I didn't want to practice ... I guess I just felt that my momentum would keep me going. But that was a mistake."

Possibly because he had learned his lesson about the difficulty handling long distance controversy by phone, Richard Williams had accompanied his family to Germany, Moscow and later to Chicago. He also apologized to Irina Spirlea for his "stupid statement" about her at the U.S. Open.

Venus played only doubles at the Ameritech Open in Chicago. She might have had a chance to qualify for the season-ending championships at Madison Square Garden in New York the following week. Only the top 16 players in the world are invited to that tournament. She also lost in the quarter-finals at the Advanta Championships in Philadelphia, and complained of homesickness.

In mid-November, Venus appeared at the Chase Championships in New York to receive an award as Newcomer of the Year on the Corel WTA Tour. With her lack of success since the U.S. Open, Venus admitted she let up afterwards. Nevertheless, Venus completed the year with an impressive 33-14 match record and had climbed to 24th in the world rankings. Her said her goal for 1998 was to get all the way to the top.

"Obviously, this year I've done okay," she said. "And next year I plan on getting better. And next year I'll be like 25th in the world. So it's not that long a way to go. You know, 24 more spaces, it's not too hard. I've worked on some things, and they still can get a lot better," she said. "There's always room for improvement for me."

In addition to making a big impression with some major wins, Venus absorbed a solid year of learning. In particular she now had a better understanding of what to do in different situations.

Venus said she was also confident her 16-year-old sister, Serena, would trail close behind her in a rapid rankings rise. To this point, Serena had seen limited competition. However, two weeks earlier in Chicago at the Ameritech she had upset highly-ranked Mary Pierce and Monica Seles.

"I think she's doing a lot better than what I did at the beginning," Venus said. "That was her fourth tournament, but she was really going at it and being serious and learning fast. She's going to come through next year."

Serena was building her own reputation. While Venus' ranking jumped from 110th to 10th in only twelve months, Serena's climb was even more dramatic. Between March 30, 1997 and March 30, 1998, she had rocketed from 453rd to 30th.

A ranking in the top 100 meant she could enter her first Grand Slam singles match the following January. "I'm just so happy that I'm in the Australian Open," she announced following her 4-6, 6-1, 6-1 quarter-final victory over Seles.

Pierce and Seles both said her style of play, while clearly built around her ability to pound the ball, surprised them. "She hit some great shots," Seles said, "and you have to attribute that to her being a great athlete."

Pam Shriver, who trained with both Venus and Serena several years ago, remembers the power the youngest Williams packed into her compact game. "Serena's forehand wasn't big on control," Shriver recalls, "but as far as power ... wow! She was just cracking the ball."

Serena's play in Chicago (she eventually lost to Lindsay Davenport in the semis) did more than get her a trip to Australia. It also placed her in the record books. She became the lowest-ranked player in WTA Tour history to defeat two top-10 players in the same tournament. She also became the lowest ranked player to defeat a player in the top five (Seles) since unranked Stephanie Rehe beat Gabriela Sabatini in 1990.

Serena's quick success again received very little coverage. People were still buzzing over Venus' performance in the U.S. Open two months earlier.

Richard Williams has long said he believed Serena would ultimately be a better player than Venus. "What makes me think Serena will be better is she has had years to sit around and watch Venus ... and see what Venus' mistakes were ... She always was a better athlete than Venus to start off with. She hits the ball harder. She returns the serve better. She places the ball better."

Their father doesn't limit his opinion on who will be

the best just within the Williams homestead. "Serena will be the best on the WTA Tour," he has also said. Whether his comments are a motivation tactic for the sisters, or a confidence-builder for Serena, no one knows.

The girls' mother refuses to take sides. "They both know they are good," Oracene Williams says. "And they just know it's a matter of time before they get it going because it's something that they work on. My girls didn't come to be on the sidelines, they come to be on top."

As with Venus, Mr. Williams has put restrictions on Serena's progress. "A lot of Serena's progress will depend on her grades," her father said. "Serena has to finish high school and take some college courses."

In October, 1997, Venus began a 10-day trip to Russia to play in the Ladies Kremlin Cup. When she first went to Olympic Stadium (where the Olympics were held in Moscow in 1980), and where the tournament was to be played, Venus got excited to see her picture posted in a Reebok booth. "... I was so happy about it because it is a good picture for once. Most every other picture I have circulating out there are double feature creature pictures!"

On the second day, Venus played Elena Likhovtseva and won 7-6 (3), 6-2. That evening she went to a VIP dinner featuring a singer and dancing.

On the third day Venus experienced something unique for her. "... It is snowing here in Russia. I have never been in snow before. I have lived in California and Florida, both sunny places..."

Venus exploded a myth on day four. "For everyone that thinks that Russia does not have toilet paper you are wrong. Whenever I told people at home that I was going to Russia they all replied: 'Oh my God, I had a friend that went to Russia and they told me that there isn't any toilet paper over there.' Imagine my dismay when everyone relayed such fallacies." At the end of her stay though, Venus said "It's been a good week. I … have enjoyed Moscow."

Venus also told her fans about the difficult questions athletes face. "The worst thing is when people ask me; 'Why didn't you win? You should have won that match.' I just say; 'Yeah, I know.' Never tell an athlete that they should have won. We know. And it hurts us 10 times more than it hurts you. You go on with your life and you say: 'Nice match, man that was epic.' But us athletes we never forget it."

Venus was thinking of going back home before long, and said, "When I get home I definitely have to get to Fort Pierce (Florida). You see I have adopted a new sport, surfing. It is so fun but unfortunately I am not so good. I must admit I pose! So, if by chance you have read in an article that I surf that statement is inaccurate. I don't surf, I wipeout. "

"I'm not looking to attain world class skills, but I would like to know that when I paddle in for a wave I will not waste it. All the time there are only guys in the lineup and they are all thinking this girl can't surf and they are right. I aim to prove them wrong even if it takes me 10 years."

Her advice to her fans was to "remember someone is always looking, and someone is always listening. This is my golden rule because I tend to do crazy things like wild dances or exaggerated impersonations when I think no one is looking, but someone really is, and I end up feeling kind of silly."

She told fans of her reading and film interests." My favorite Shakespearean play is *Macbeth*. I have read *Hamlet* and *Romeo and Juliet*, but I really don't like those. I haven't read the other tragedies yet like *King Lear* or *Othello* nor have I read any of the Histories. My favorite books are *The Shawshank Redemption*, *The Hobbit* and *The Lord of the Rings* trilogy by J.R.R. Tolkein. My favorite movie is *Shawshank Redemption*."

Chapter 6:
Sibling Love And Rivalry

In 1990, on a hard court in Arcadia, California, Serena had to play her older sister Venus in the 10-and-under final in Junior tennis. Venus, who even then towered over Serena, whomped her younger sister pretty badly.

From the time they were little, Venus and Serena have been buddies, best friends really. Serena, the baby of the family, always seemed to be at Venus' side or sitting in the stands rooting for her older sibling.

Although Venus got most of the press coverage, Serena herself would soon emerge as a tennis force to be reckoned with. If Venus was an ascending planet, Serena was a rising star. On the women's tour they stuck together. They also stuck up for one another. After beating Anne Miller in straight sets in a first-round match at the Evert Cup Indian Wells in March 1997, Venus greeted a stunned Miller at the net. She told her, "You beat my sister. I owed you."

Fellow players are well-aware of their close ties. "She

Venus and Serena smile for the camera before their quarterfinal match at the Italian Open clay court tournament in May, 1998. Venus won, 6-4, 6-2.

seems to be going all the time with her sister, her mom, too," said Monica Seles. "That's what family is for. They stay in their own little separate group."

After Venus' quarter-final win over Sandrine Testud at the U.S. Open in 1997, Venus and Serena locked arms in a stadium hallway. They began singing and dancing as they walked, two sisters having great fun. Venus looked the same way she does after a victory.

The sisters also shared similar tastes in music. At home, they listen to the rock bands Rage Against the Machine, Rancid and The Foo Fighters. In a shed near their house there's a drum set neither have had time to learn how to play. "We were going to have jam sessions in there," Serena told a reporter from *Tennis* magazine in the summer of 1997. Like her sister, Serena also has a guitar.

Also like Venus, Serena loves to surf. "I was at the beach and there was this program going on for little kids," Serena explained. "They all had surfboards and I had a rotten, ugly, horrible, nasty, funky boogie board. I got a short board, which allows me to rip and shred, but Venus went crazy and got a 10-footer."

They both think skateboarders are cool but in-line skaters are posers. "We don't like in-line skaters, we don't like people who like in-line skaters and we don't talk about in-line skating," said Serena.

Despite their closeness, in many ways they are as different as night and day, especially in appearance. For one thing Venus, at 6'2", is a good four inches taller than Serena. While Venus is lean, Serena is stockier, solid like a rock. Venus looks like an queen; Serena like a warrior with her muscular, almost chiseled, physique. The only similarities they seem to have are the braces on their teeth which become visible when they break into broad grins.

There are other differences besides physical characteristics. "With Venus, everything comes so easy, whether it's athletic or academic," their mother has said. "With Serena, it comes a little harder, but that makes her work harder, too. She's more of a stick-to-it person."

Unlike Venus, who grasps things quickly yet tires at the same speedy pace, Serena needs time, whether it's learning how to hit a forehand passing shot, or warming up to strangers. Where Venus sometimes hangs back on the court, Serena is more aggressive, fearless and offense-oriented. Serena's middle name, Billie Jean King once joked, is "Forward."

While Venus will battle her father playing video games, Serena will more likely be found curled up with a book. She often has one of the family dogs in her lap. The family used to have another dog besides Star, Queen and Chase. Princess accidentally drowned in one of the lakes on the Williams property.

"I would always throw her in the water, and she would always swim back," said Serena. "She was a homebody; she never went anywhere. She loved us. She loved everybody. One day, we were looking everywhere for her, and my Dad saw her here, floating in the water." As a result, Serena refers to the smaller of the two lakes as "Lake Inferior."

Serena and Venus like to play games – with each other. In an interview appearing in *Seventeen* magazine, Serena described Venus as "very, very tall." Venus responded, "Well, Serena's pretty wide." Then they both started giggling.

Noted Venus; "Serena knows exactly what she wants in life." Serena responded, playing along, "When I was younger I wanted to be just like Venus."

Venus claims Serena used to steal things from her when they were little. Venus also said Serena is "kind of a perfectionist, though not neurotic or psychotic."

Venus said she tries to take care of her younger sibling. "I'm a good sister," Venus says. "I let her sleep while I'm driving."

Serena hopes someday to become a veterinarian. She graduated from a private high school in Florida in May 1998. Eventually, she'll enroll in a local college. (Her father doesn't want her traveling and taking correspondence courses.)

Venus graduated from high school in 1997, (with a 3.75 grade point average, she reports). When she had the time, she took some classes at Palm Beach Community College, but wasn't enrolled by early 1998. "I promised my dad I'd go to college, and I will, absolutely," she said after she and Serena won a first-round doubles match at the Australian Open in January 1998. "I'll take architecture and design classes."

Serena and Venus seem to be up for almost anything. During the U.S. Open in 1997, they visited Shea Stadium, home of the New York Mets, and took batting practice. Neither would agree the other hit better, although Venus, who tried hitting both left and right-handed, managed to smack one ball past second base.

Both girls said they had fun as they stood side by side, holding hands and fielding questions from the media. Oracene Williams stood back a few feet as the girls faced a large contingent of reporters and assorted TV cameras and microphones. "It's not too bad because I know when to say 'no,'" Mrs. Williams said of all the media attention. Still, it was hard for her to see her youngest children growing up.

Naturally, the girls are excited whenever they win a match. Perhaps the most excited they've ever been was when as part of a promotion of the IGA Classic they got to appear on their favorite TV program, an unlikely game show called "Supermarket Sweeps." They were able to throw $485 worth of groceries into two carts within the allotted time. "It was like realizing a dream," Venus told *Vogue* magazine. Added Serena, "It was wonderful. I could do that, like, every day."

Venus and Serena once admitted they had always had a childhood fantasy to be fire fighters. They fulfilled their childhood dreams when they toured Station House No. 2 in downtown Miami on a Sunday morning in March, 1998.

Serena climbed into the driver's seat of the fire truck and took it for a short ride. They also tested some the equipment and even donned the clothes the fire fighters would wear in case of a real emergency, including oxygen tanks and masks.

"Serena and I came here to learn what other people do every day when they go to work," said Venus. "We are so committed to tennis and it's really great to see other people as committed to their work as we are to tennis. Especially when it's people like these firefighters who save people's lives."

Around the same time, Serena accompanied her father to Atlanta for the Super Show, the sporting industry's trade exhibition. At the show, sportswear giant Puma announced it had signed Serena to a five-year, multi-million dollar contract to promote its line of clothes and shoes.

The visit to Atlanta had a dual purpose. In nearby College Park, Georgia, Serena visited the Burdette Junior Tennis Academy where it was announced Serena would be "adopting" their program.

"When I made the announcement they all went crazy," said Ernie Peterson, who started the Burdette Academy in 1979. "It gives our program some real credence after being out there in the trenches for so long. Now we can touch more kids' lives."

As part of the adoption, Serena plans to visit the academy three times a year, working with the academy's 30 players. "I always wanted to be a part of any program that helps kids because I used to be one myself," said Serena. Quickly realizing she herself was only 16 years old, she added: "Wait, what am I saying here?"

Serena's father was quick to point out that the program was not intended to become a farm for future tennis pros. He repeated what he had said so often before.

"I'll make sure kids in our program have an average of 'B+' or above. We push education more than anything else."

The Burdette program is made up predominantly of African-American players. Since it began, 41 players have received tennis scholarships. The selection of Burdette meant that Serena and Venus had adopted similar programs in 18 different states. Like her sister, Serena was giving back to the community.

The Williams sisters had been so mature in handling their responsibilities, their father said, he allowed them to go off to tournaments without their "coach." In January 1998, he said good-bye as they boarded a jet bound for Australia. But their mother was traveling with them.

After they left, their father said he had mixed feelings. Despite the success of his daughters, Richard Williams wondered sometimes if he has gone about things the right way. He thinks track and field would have been better for his daughters because "they would have stayed in school." "If I had to do it over," he said, "I wouldn't put them into tennis."

Chapter 7:
Rising Superstars

It didn't take long in the 1998 Corel WTA Tour for both Venus and Serena to spring surprises. Venus, overcoming cramps, defeated top-ranked Martina Hingis 3-6, 6-4, 7-5. "It took me four times to beat Martina," she said afterwards. "When I lose to a player, the next time I try to change my game and cut down on the unforced errors... Usually I am a power hitter, I power myself out of the match. Against a player like Martina that likes to take the pace off the a ball and lift it back, you really can't do that."

Shortly thereafter, Serena used the same tactic to knock off highly regarded sixteen-year-old Mirjana Lucic. Serena said she got motivated during the change over in the second set when a fan yelled out, "Hey, Serena! Venus just won!" "I wanted to jump up and down, but then I remembered that I was playing my own match and that it was time to get serious. It gave me a jolt and I started playing better."

In the next round, Venus defeated Maggie Maleeva of

Bulgaria while Serena upset Sandrine Testud. The beat went on.

Venus and Serena both made it into the semi-finals. Serena put together a masterful 1-6, 7-5, 7-5 comeback on a gimpy knee against third-ranked Lindsay Davenport. Soon after, Venus beat Maggie Maleeva 6-2, 6-2.

Serena showed great courage in her quarter-final win. Limping on her bandaged right knee and losing 1-3 in the second set, Serena took a 10-minute injury time-out. She not only used the time to tend to her knee, but to "regroup my thoughts, stay calm and take time to think everything through, point by point." When they returned, Serena immediately broke Davenport's service.

She then fashioned her victory by cutting down on the errors that had cost her the first set. She suddenly started ripping winners down the lines and into the corners from both sides, and watched Davenport dig herself deeper into trouble with double-faults and mistakes. "This is my most satisfying win," Serena said. "She's the highest ranked player I have beaten."

Venus watched her sister's comeback and called it amazing, but in someways expected. "I know Serena never gives up, and I know she finds a way to win," she said.

The sisters' victories meant they could end up facing each other in the final of the tournament. First, though, Serena had to beat Arantxa Sanchez Vicario in the semis, and Venus, Ai Sugiyama. If they were to meet, the sisters said people shouldn't expect them to take it easy on one another. "She's my sister, but I want to win," Serena said. Venus echoed that sentiment. "I'm trying to get my first title, too," she said. "So I'm going to try to win. I don't care who it is."

The confrontation was not to be for the time being. Venus won, and Serena lost. But it would not be long before the sisters would meet in competition.

The following week, both sisters won their opening round of the Australian Open in Melbourne. The Australian Open is the first Grand Slam event of the year. Venus Williams won 6-3, 6-0 over Alexia Dechaume-Balleret. Serena came back after being down a set against sixth-seeded Irina Spirlea to win, 6-7 (5-7), 6-3, 6-1. The victories set up the confrontation they barely missed in Sydney. They were to play each other in the next round.

Serena and Venus don't play full matches when they practice against each other, but there's no holding back in their "scrimmages." "She smoked me a few weeks ago," Serena once recalled. "But then the next time we played, I smoked her a little. We go at it pretty hard. We just don't keep score." She added, "My forehand is better than hers, her backhand may be a bit better than mine."

Suddenly, comments that Serena would surpass Venus started being echoed by several players, including Lindsay Davenport and Arantxa Sanchez Vicario (who had beaten Venus in the final the previous week in

Sydney.) Serena, they said, had a better serve, was more consistent on ground strokes, and seemed to hit the ball more crisply.

Serena, so used to being in the background, ate up all the attention. "I like it when my opponents fear me," the younger Williams said. "However, I don't think Venus has a reason to fear me. I have no reason to fear her also."

"I guess I always imagined Serena and I as No. 1 and No. 2," Venus said. "I didn't exactly imagine playing each other, although that would be a possibility. I feel that young Serena is going to want to beat on me, so I better be ready."

Before the match, their father predicted that no matter what happened, his daughters would be enjoying themselves. "I think they're going to have a lot of fun," he said from his Florida home. "I'm also glad I'm not there to see it. I think the referee would have to kick me out because I'd be having too much fun, saying 'Girl, you go at it.'"

The much-ballyhooed battle between sister and sister turned out to be less exciting than everyone hoped. Venus beat Serena 7-6 (7-4), 6-1 in a somewhat sloppy match. Whether they were too respectful of each other, or knew each other too well, the sisters failed to push each other. Serena double-faulted on her serves eight times, Venus five. Serena whacked 42 errors, Venus 34. Each held serve only twice in the first set.

Afterwards, Venus and Serena clasped hands and

hugged. They then turned to the crowd, hands held tightly, and bowed together. When they left the court, they were still holding hands. They then received the loudest applause of the day.

"Was it fun? I think it would have been great fun if it were the final," Venus said. "It was a match. A tough match."

Their former coach said this was just the first of many battles between the two sisters. "They're probably going to have to play each other 20 times before they retire," said Rick Macci.

After beating Serena, Venus then defeated Amelie Mauresmo and Patty Schnyder. She then lost to Lindsay Davenport, whom Serena had beaten one week earlier.

But there was one victory for the Williams' household. Teaming up with Justin Gemelstob, Venus won the mixed-doubles championship. It was her first Grand Slam title of any kind. In the finals Venus and Justin defeated Byril Suk and Helena Sukova in straight sets. Although Venus was happy with the results, winning her first singles title still eluded her. Soon she would correct that.

Before they left Australia, Venus and Serena cooked up a new idea; a battle of the sexes. They approached officials of the men's ATP Tour to line up one-set challenges against male players ranked in the 200s.

"I decided I wanted to be part of the (men's) tour,"

Serena said. "I'm looking forward to it, I'm really ready, It'll be fun." Venus said she wanted to play for pride and maybe one ATP computer point.

Australian Open referee Peter Bellenger said he had no concerns about the contests taking place on an outside court as long as the players went through the official channels and booked the court for practice.

Germany's Karsten Braasch, 203rd on the men's tour, took up a challenge to play Serena in a set Sunday, but rain forced them to postpone their plan. On Tuesday, the sisters played Braasch on Court 12 in the boondocks of the Australian Open complex. A few hundred fans and players wandered by and watched along with a crowd of media. There was no umpire, no linesmen, no ball boys, no scoreboard. Only pride was at stake.

The sisters discovered quickly that they were no match for the men on the ATP Tour. Serena fell 6-1, Venus 6-2. They played as intensely as they could, while Braasch seemed to have a relatively easy time of it.

"I didn't know it would be that hard," said Serena. "I hit shots that would have been winners on the WTA Tour, and he got to them easily." That didn't stop her from boasting that, she'd beat him the following year. "First I have to pump some weight, " she added.

Asked if she might not want to take on players on the senior tour, or retired men, as Billie Jean King had done against 1939 Wimbledon champion Bobby Riggs in their much ballyhooed "Battle of the Sexes" in 1973, Venus shook her beaded head. "I'm going for the young guns," she said.

In March 1998, Venus won her first Corel WTA Tour singles title by defeating Joannette Kruger of South Africa 6-3, 6-2 in the final at the IGA Tennis Classic in Oklahoma City. Naturally, Venus was excited afterwards. "Winning the tournament means a lot to me, and it's one I'll always remember," she exclaimed. "I can say it all started back in Oklahoma City."

The win wasn't easy. After Venus took a 4-1 lead in the first set, Kruger came back to get within 3-4. Venus was able to hold her off. In the second set, Venus jumped out to a 3-1 lead. Again, Kruger climbed back to within 2-3. However, as she had done in the first set, Venus won the final two games to secure the victory. Kruger became more and more tired as the match wore on. "It was a tough match," she said. "I think I ran twice as much as she did."

Venus collected the first prize of $27,000. The good news wasn't over just yet, though. After capturing her singles title, Venus joined her sister, Serena, in the doubles final. (In the singles draw, Serena had lost in the quarter-finals.) The sister duo defeated Catalina Cristea from Romania and Kristine Kunce from Australia, 7-5, 6-2 for their first career women's doubles title. The Williams sisters broke Cristea, when she was serving at 5-6, to capture the first set. After taking a quick 3-0 lead in the second set, they pulled away and never looked back. "I felt really excited after winning," Serena said. "It's pretty special to play with Venus."

With the doubles title, 16-year-old Serena reached a milestone. She became the youngest champion in IGA Tennis Classic history. The previous record holder? Venus, who had held the distinction since her singles championship of a few days earlier.

There was one more quick stop before the girls got to play near home. At the Evert Cup Indian Wells in California, Venus lost in the finals to her rival, Martina Hingis. Martina blew her away in the first set 6-0 before Venus recovered in the second set, but still lost, 6-7. Serena sat out the singles event in order to focus on doubles.

The girls made it to the semi-finals in doubles before losing a tough three-set battle. The winners? Mirjana Lucic and Martina Hingis.

Even though she had lost, Venus still insisted that she and Serena would rule the world of women's tennis in the near future. "That's our plan," she said. "We don't see anyone else – or we don't want anyone else to try to stop us."

"She said it again?" asked Hingis when the comment was told to her. " … Nothing new anymore. So far she's not. I mean, one day, if I'm probably not playing anymore, she could get there."

Before leaving Indian Wells, Martina Hingis was still

stinging from Venus' earlier comment. Firmly entrenched at Number One, Martina said the Williams sisters didn't stand a chance at consistently beating her for the remainder of the year. "Venus beat me in Sydney, but she hasn't beaten me at a big tournament. Of course they're maturing and they're getting older and better, but they still have to show they can get the results at the big tournaments." Maturing? Martina herself was only 17.

There was a comment from another player earlier that also may have played on the Williams sisters' minds. It came from the pretty 16-year-old Russian blonde. Anna Kournikouva. Her rapid climb up the rankings rivaled that of Venus and Serena. "I have watched both Serena and Venus play, and they're not that good. They don't know how to play points or how to win." It was time to go home to Florida.

The Tennis Center at Crandon Park on the island of Key Biscayne is an attractive, bowl-shaped facility. All the playing surfaces are bright green. Circling the Stadium court, where the featured matches are played, black boards with light green writing advertise the sponsors' products. Key Biscayne is only a few miles south of the Williams' home in Palm Beach Gardens.

Crandon Park seats 14,000 spectators, and for every match Venus and Serena played, the seats were nearly filled. Seated in a box near courtside were the sisters' family. Even their father Richard was there, often pacing the aisles. It was an important tournament for 1998. "The Lipton is the biggest event after the Grand Slams," said tennis commentator Cliff Drysdale.

Both girls had little trouble in the early rounds. Serena beat Denisa Chladkova, Irina Spirlea, Barbara Paulus, and Patty Schnyder. Only Schynyder won a set off of her.

Venus played even better. She beat Tatiana Panova, Olga Barabanschikova, Rita Grande and Silvia Farina in straight sets. Only Rita Grande won as many as four games from Venus.

When Venus polished off Panova, she hurt her left knee in the second set. Afterwards Venus wouldn't discuss her injury but said it wouldn't affect her championship run. She would wear a wrap on it for the rest of the tournament.

Venus hit the fastest serve ever clocked at the Lipton by a woman, at 122 miles-per-hour . That tied her for 12th fastest by a man during the tournament. Her serve was only one mile-per-hour slower than that of tennis legend Andre Agassi. The second fastest woman's serve was by Serena, at 110 mph.

In the quarter-finals, Serena was to face the Number One seed, Martina Hingis; the thorn in her sister's side. It would be the first time Serena would play her in a singles match. If Serena won, it would set up another showdown with Venus. First, though, there was something else on Serena's mind: school work. "I might have to go to summer school because I'm getting behind in Algebra II," she said.

By match time, Serena felt ready to compete. She had the shots to keep up with Martina Hingis, and she had already proven that she could run down any ball that came over the net at The Lipton. However, Serena's nerves were not calm enough. Martina won 6-3, 1-6, 7-6 (7-4) advancing to the semi-finals against Venus. Serena came within one point of winning, but Martina was too sly.

At 5-4 in the third set, Hingis called for a trainer on the changeover. "I think she was very nervous, so she called the trainer to get some time, get some coaching," Serena said. "I'm not sure what she did."

Hingis said all the running in the very physical match had exhausted her legs, and she started cramping. Martina also knew that calling a trainer might prove nerve-wracking to a less experienced player. "My legs were hurting," she said. "But you also think a little bit about that (the psychological effect on her opponent)."

During the three-minute injury time-out, Williams sat on her bench – a few feet from where her father watched from the first row – and concentrated, she said. Then she lost eight of the next ten points, to allow Hingis to go ahead 6-5, and had to hold serve just to reach a tiebreaker. "I think I tried too hard," Williams said of the final few minutes of the match.

After the match, Serena rushed to pick up her bag and take the rubber bands out of her hair while giving a quick wave to the appreciative crowd. She was obviously upset. She brushed by a crowd of kids seeking autographs. "I feel I could have done better," she said later. "I don't think I played so well. I guess I should be satisfied, but I don't know."

Hingis now had a 5-1 record against the Williams sisters. As for Serena, she said, "She's going to be a tough opponent in the future." What she didn't say was, "but not now, and the same goes for her sister," but no doubt she was thinking it.

Venus and Martina Hingis were both 17 years old at the Lipton. Besides that, they had very little in common. Venus is from the USA, Martina is from Europe and now lives in Switzerland. Venus is tall, (6' 2"), Martina is of average height (5' 6") One was named for a tennis star (Martina Navratilova), the other for the evening star. One wears a ribbon in her hair and the other wears beads in her braids. Martina laughs with opponents, the other is all business.

It was expected that the other players on the tour would root for Hingis, a popular player with other pros, and not Williams, who is perceived as stand-offish. Lindsay Davenport, one of the players who has mentioned Williams' chilly locker room demeanor, said Hingis is a fun opponent. "I think she has the best attitude of any top player that's ever been there," she said.

The two did have one other thing in common. They

very well could be the present and future of women's tennis. "This could become a rivalry that could dominate the Women's Tour," said tennis commentator Cliff Drysdale prior to their semi-final match.

Said Pam Shriver; "This is their sixth meeting in 12 months. People compare it to a rivalry that began 20 years ago – Martina Navratilova and Chris Evert. But they played 80 matches, so these two would have to play six times for 13 years to equal that."

Venus appeared to be on a mission from the first point of the match. Venus marched quickly to and from her chair during changeovers. She hit winners from the baseline that even the speedy Hingis couldn't reach. Then she unveiled a new weapon. She displayed a wicked overhead shot, including two in a row during the final game of the first set. Each time, Venus leaped into the air on the run, her long limbs fully stretched out. She clobbered the ball each time, sending it on one hop into the stands behind Martina.

Venus won the match relatively easily, 6-2, 5-7, 6-2. The victory could have been more lopsided, but in the second set, Venus squandered a 3-0 lead and three match points. "I was just much too tight and much too pumped," she said. "After I lost that game, it was like, 'Wow, how could I have done that?'" After she won, Venus broke into her patented dance step in celebration.

Martina conceded she couldn't match Venus' power. "She's taller than me," Hingis said. "What can I do about that? I know I can't hit the ball as hard as she can. It's difficult to play the Williams family two matches in a row," Hingis said with a laugh.

By winning, Venus avenged a 6-0, 7-6 loss to Hingis at Indian Wells two weeks earlier, but Hingis still led the rivalry 4-2. "This time last year I was No. 211 in the world," Williams said, laughing. "I'm going to keep moving up."

Venus didn't have long to celebrate after beating Martina. Waiting in the wings for her was another up-and-comer even younger than her; Anna Kournikouva. Anna was blond and beautiful. She was so popular with male fans that earlier in the year, in Sydney, Australia, a fight broke out in the stands over Kournikova's sweaty towel. But her looks had nothing to do with her tennis. Anna had already knocked off three top-ranked players in the Lipton to make it to the finals.

After defeating two-time champ Arantxa Sanchez Vicario to make it to the finals, Anna said, "It shows everybody that I can play. It didn't just happen one time unexpectedly. I proved to everybody that I can play good tennis a lot of matches in a row."

Venus was in a novel position. With all the top contenders already eliminated, Venus, for the first time, was the favorite.

All the talk of someday being on top had come to a head. Venus could no longer just talk about what she was going to do someday, where she was going to be in the rankings in the future. All the talk was over. It was in the past. It was put up or shut up time, and the pressure on Venus was awful. On top of that, she was about to break into the top ten. That meant more players would be gunning for her. Anna was only the first.

Venus and Anna would be facing each other for the first time. Both were noted for hitting with power from the baseline and for only occasionally charging the net. The taller Williams had the stronger serve, while Kournikova was more agile.

After years of promise – and boasting – it was time to find out if Venus was truly great or famous only because of her unusual beaded hair and long legs.

By early in the second set, Kournikova was ahead, offseting Venus' power game with a variety of off-speed shots and precise angles keeping her off-balance. Things were getting worse for Venus.

Could Venus' newfound success come crashing down at the hands of a girl one year younger than she? How could she ever win one of the big "Grand Slam" tennis tournaments like the U.S. Open in New York or Wimbledon in London, if she couldn't handle the stress in Key Biscayne? Spectators had to wonder; would Venus Williams rise to the occasion, or come crashing down to earth?

But suddenly, Venus evened the score at 30-all in the

third game of the second set, on a long corner-to-corner shot. After a grueling point that included over 20 volleys, Kournikova was bent at the waist, her racquet held loosely in her hand. She was clearly out of breath. To make matters worse, Anna had taken a patented Venus Williams rocket shot to the body. Fom that point on, her rests increased while the precision of her shots decreased. The subtle change was all Venus needed. She ran Kournikova even harder and came storming back in the second and third sets to win the biggest title of her career. The final score was 2-6, 6-4, 6-1. Serena sat court-side as Venus carved up Kournikova in the third set and you could sense that she, too, wished she was out there on the Stadium Court.

When it was over, Venus raised both hands in triumph before doing her dance. Dejected, Anna hit the ground repeatedly with her racquet.

It was Venus' career-high and a sign of her desire to win. She celebrated by dashing up the stands and over several sections of seats to hug her mom and sisters. Her father had moved to the front row carrying his erasable marker board for the final point. He jumped up and down in circles with the board over his head when she won. Her victory check totaled $235,000.

Venus put the victory in its proper Williams-family perspective. "When I win, everyone wins – Serena wins, my mom wins," smiled Venus. "It's just good for all of us. It helps Serena too, because when I win, I can tell her what I did to win, what kind of experiences I had on the court. It helps her a lot, so she'll know what to do."

A stress injury to her knee caused Venus to drop out of the Bausch & Lomb Championships at Amelia Island Plantation in northern Florida in April. "After the finals, she was so stiff and so sore she had to be helped around by two people," Said Bob Arrix, the Bausch & Lomb tournament chairman. "This is one of those things. Playing on will only aggravate it."

Arrix said Venus had been rehabilitating the knee twice a day but, it hadn't responded to the treatment as well as doctors hoped. "The doctors told her if she doesn't rest it she'll damage it," Arrix said.

By May 1998, Venus' knee was feeling much better and she was raring to get back into action. Now that their father eased up a bit in limiting how many tournaments they could play, Venus and Serena headed for the Italian Open.

With two tournament titles, Venus now expected to win every event she entered. It just wasn't to be. In her first tournament since recovering from tenonitis in her left knee, Venus made it to the finals of the Italian Open, but lost soundly to Martina Hingis.

First, though, she got to play Serena in the quarter-finals. "When I saw the draw I was disappointed because I was looking forward to a final or semi-final meeting," said Serena, who was now ranked 31st.

To reach the sister matchup, Serena beat four-time Italian Open champion Conchita Martinez on center court. Meanwhile, Venus beat Alexandra Fusai, the Frenchwoman who upset the second-seeded Jana Novotna the previous afternoon on the grandstand court. While Venus and Serena dashed across the red clay courts, Oracene Williams, wearing a warm-up suit and sneakers, ran across the concourse attempting to watch both daughters. "I think I covered more ground than they did," she said.

In their second meeting on the WTA tour, Venus again defeated her sister. The Williams family showdown lacked excitement as Venus won, 6-4, 6-2. "The first time was different," said Serena, explaining the lack of emotion by the two sisters. For the first time in Rome, their mother was able to remain seated.

"I was a little disappointed," Serena said after the match. "I went out there really wanting to win this time."

"I think Serena knows what she needs to do to beat me," said her big sister. "But I'd have to make a lot of mistakes."

Venus then beat Arantxa Sanchez Vicario in the semi-finals. Up next, she had to face Martina Hingis in a showdown.

The first set between Venus and Hingis was marked by service breaks and erratic play. Hingis regained her poise quickly and took control. She ran off the last three games and wrapped up the set in 37 minutes. Midway

Parents Richard and Oracene Williams and a beaded Serena watch from the stands as Venus plays Elena Wagner in the first round of the 1998 U.S. Open

through the third set, Hingis was back in control and on her way to the title.

Venus offered no excuses, unwilling to complain of the knee ailment that forced her to take an injury time-out during her semi-final victory over Arantxa Sanchez Vicario. She did complain a little about the schedule. In particular, she was miffed over having to play a two-hour doubles match with Serena following her semi-final singles victory. The Williams sisters lost to Virgina Ruano Pascual of Spain and Paola Suarez of Argentina

2-6, 6-4, 7-5 in the doubles semi-finals.

"I would play singles in the afternoon, and wait around all day to play doubles. I'd get to the hotel late, eat and try to sleep. Maybe next year, I won't enter the doubles."

"I was surprised at the way she played," said Martina. "She was fighting. She didn't give up until the end."

Even though clay playing surfaces were not her favorite, Venus was pleased. "I thought I brought the level of my game up," she said. "At first it was hard for me to get my footwork straight on the clay, I just don't play on it enough. Near the end of the week, I was able to do that better and better." There was one consolation. By reaching the final, Venus moved up two places to Number 7 in the WTA rankings.

Martina said Venus was starting to play like she's Number 2. Tennis observers declared the two were becoming the hottest rivalry in women's tennis, reminiscent of former rivalries of Chris Evert-Martina Navratilova and Monica Seles-Steffi Graf. Martina said there was little doubt that she and Venus would be challenging each other frequently in the future. "Venus is the toughest teenager of all," she said.

Before the French Open later in May, Martina planned to take a week off at home in Zurich before going to Paris. For Hingis, hopping around Europe is the next thing to being at home. "It's only a one-hour flight to Zurich from the tournaments," she said.

For Venus, it was a little tougher. She returned to Florida to rest before heading back to Europe.

Venus said she looked forward to her second appearance in Paris and only her third-ever tournament on clay. "I was having good time on the clay at Roland Garros, (the popular name for the French Open) playing well and sliding well – I just couldn't win," she said of her 1997 experience. "Now I'm a smarter player, with more to offer, but maybe my opponents don't want those things offered to them. Still, I'll have a good time at Roland Garros."

Paris is a city of high fashion. Venus and Serena are anything but that. Venus wears a necklace made of dice that spells out "Venus No. 1." Serena wears a Goofy watch on one wrist and a "Cat in the Hat" watch on the other when she plays.

Venus and Serena seem to enjoy their non-traditional images. "We're different than what has normally come to tennis in the past," she said. "We try to make it exciting."

In the first round of the French Open, Venus was all business throughout the match and overwhelmed Tamarine Tanasugarn of Thailand 6-3, 6-1. At one point, fans giggled as Williams slid for a shot on the soft clay and ended up in a split - her long legs spread wide like a gymnast. Venus remained expressionless. Only after the final point of the next-to-last game did Venus smile. She pulled back on the power for a moment and hit a delicate drop shot that trickled over the net for a winner. She then turned 180 degrees and smiled quickly at Serena, sitting in the stands. "I think the only people that are going to run that down are Serena and me," she said later, explaining the smile. Five points later, the match was over and Williams was signing autographs.

Venus was also overpowering in a 6-0, 6-2 second-round victory against Ai Sugiyama. Venus won the first eight games. She never allowed Sugiyama, ranked 19th in the world and considered one of the most dangerous unseeded players at the French Open, to win any of her seven service games.

As luck would have it, Venus, with blue and white beads in her hair, had to play Martina Hingis in the quarter-finals. A large crowd showed up for the early afternoon match between them. Venus' erratic playing left the spectators murmuring with surprise more than erupting in cheers.

All match long, Venus failed to counter Hingis' patience and precision on the tricky red clay, made even trickier in windy conditions. Venus' powerful groundstrokes often were misdirected; she committed 38 unforced errors, 10 more than Martina. Hingis won the match with relative ease, 6-3, 6-4.

Afterwards, wearing a navy blue T-shirt, Venus stepped up to the podium, holding her head just as high as usual, and offered a brief pose for the camera. When she spoke, Venus was more somber than usual. "I think I'm going to have to get a little more serious," she said. "It's probably good for me to lose, so I can really see what I'm doing wrong ... Now, I can look at myself and say, 'Venus, you're not there.'"

There was one consolation in Paris. Venus and her mixed doubles partner, Justin Gamelstob, won the mixed doubles title.

As for Serena, she had little success in Paris. In her last match, Serena was within two points of victory against Sanchez Vicario before losing in three sets. The match was marred by outbursts of temper by both players. Afterwards, Sanchez Vicario accused Serena of "failing to show respect."

However, Serena was becoming more comfortable on the tour and her relationships with many of the other players were good. "I think Serena is hysterical," said Lindsay Davenport. "She's a very funny girl and very outgoing." Davenport noted Venus still didn't talk to any other players. "I think her sister is very nice-- her sister talks to anybody."

Before they left Paris, Venus and Serena said good-bye to the French fans, adding that they'd be back next year. The French people loved them for saying that, especially since they said it in French.

The Eastbourne Championships in England serve as a grass-surface tune-up for Wimbledon. In her first match, Serena beat Naoko Sawamatsu 6-4, 7-5 in the opening round. Watching in the stands were Venus and her mother, who was on crutches after breaking her left ankle in a fall at the house the Williams family rented at Wimbledon.

Serena had her own trouble with her footing on the unfamiliar grass surface. "It was kind of slippery out there, and I really don't like falling at all," she said. "But I came to the net more in the first set than I have this whole year."

Venus wasn't so fortunate. Natasha Zvereva spoiled her 18th birthday by routing her 6-2, 6-1. Playing in a cold, blustery wind, Venus had trouble adapting her game to the grass that had been removed from the old No. 1 court at Wimbledon and transported to Eastbourne.

Zvereva dominated the match by mixing up her game and taking the pace off the ball. Venus decided to rally from the baseline and rarely came to the net or played volleys. In the final game, Venus double-faulted on her serve and ended the match with a forehand that sailed over the baseline. "I was very inconsistent and didn't play well," she said. "I played poorly. That's the word."

Venus had practiced on grass for only two days before the match, and felt she had not approached it in the right way. "I've learned that I'm going to have to practice harder and be more serious in my practices," she said. "I wasn't overconfident, but in practice I should play every point as if I were in a match. Sometimes when I practice I try a lot of different things instead of really focusing."

That it came on her birthday didn't bother Venus at all. As a Jehovah's Witness, she doesn't celebrate it anyway.

Serena lasted one more match than her older sister. She reached the quarter-finals by beating No. 8 seed Ai Sugiyama of Japan 6-2, 7-5, but then lost to Arantxa Sanchez Vicario.

For the really big tournament, Serena decided to be more outlandish in the color combinations of her beads than Venus. "I'm going for as many colors as I can for Wimbledon. I really don't like that you have to wear all white."

By the luck of the draw, Venus and Serena Williams were grouped in the same bracket. That meant they could play each other in the fourth match of the tournament. They would both have to get that far for that to happen. Serena reacted to the possibility with one word, "cool."

Almost immediately there was a minor controversy. "Yesterday I had this cookie," Venus declared. "And I had to go for something for Mom. I come back and the cookie is gone," said a clearly exasperated Venus.

"I said: 'Serena, did you eat the cookie?' 'Yes I did,' she told me. I said: 'I would appreciate it if you didn't do that any more.'

"Something like that can be very irritating. It's not the first time she took my cookie. It's a long history. It dates back to '91."

In the first round, Venus beat Jana Nejedly of Canada and Serena beat Laura Golarsa. It almost didn't happen. Venus was within minutes of forfeiting after arriving late. She said she had become lost on the way to the stadium.

Fans were shocked by the astonishing physique of Serena Williams. Wearing a sleeveless dress, her rippling shoulder muscles were visible from the top row.

In the second round it was time for Venus to flex her muscles. She slammed a serve at 125 mph, the fastest ever recorded in women's tennis. When told of her sister's feat, Serena said, "Jeepers. Wow. I'm behind. I don't know if I can catch up with that. She's much bigger than I am. She's taller and she might have more power."

Venus learned of the achievement after her match from Serena, who was told about it by the media. "I wasn't going for any big ones today," Venus said, "so that was a surprise."

The serve, which came on an ace in the third game of the second set, broke the previous record of 123 mph by Brenda Schultz-McCarthy at Wimbledon the previous year. Williams' previous best was 122 mph at the Lipton Championships this year. (Serena's best is 112 mph.) The fastest serve in men's history was 143 mph by Greg Rusedski at the 1997 U.S. Open.

Venus expects her serving speed will continue to

improve. "I've just turned 18, so I'm just going to get stronger," she said. "I would imagine that my peak would be at 22 or 23. In the last year, I gained 9 mph on my serve."

Both girls easily beat their second round opponents. Serena won a battle of 16-year-olds, sweeping the final nine games to eliminate Mirjana Lucic 6-3, 6-0. Venus beat Barbara Schett 6-1, 6-2.

After Serena beat highly regarded Lucic, Venus said, "Serena is definitely a juggernaut." And how, she was asked, do you stop a juggernaut? "Just become a bigger one yourself," Venus said. "I guess you have to become a nemesis."

The more she played, the more Serena liked playing on grass. "When I first was hitting on it, I didn't like it," she said. "Now I love it. Grass helps my game on other surfaces, because usually I don't attack. It will help me come to the net more." The girls were having fun. Unfortunately, it wouldn't last.

Serena retired from her third-round match with Virginia Ruano-Pascual, hobbling with a leg injury and trailing 7-5, 4-1. She had injured herself while slipping on the slick grass (the grass she was starting to love) during the middle of the set.

"I could have carried on if I wanted but I have to think about the future," she said. "I don't want to hurt myself over something silly and be out for maybe two months just because I didn't stop." Serena had been heavily favored to beat Ruano-Pascual to set up a fourth-round showdown against Venus. "We were getting pretty excited about facing each other again," Serena said. "It was going to give something exciting for England for once."

Serena was clearly disappointed. "I expected to go all the way. I guess I just won't be able to this year. In the future, I definitely see myself as one of the champions."

Serena kept a straight face when she said she had done sister Venus a huge favor by withdrawing. "Venus now has a better chance of doing well. In fact, I will give her a couple of tips for her next match."

Although she and Venus decided to pull out of the women's doubles competition, Serena did manage to win her first Grand Slam title before she left Wimbledon. With a few days of extra rest and therapy on her leg, she and partner Max Mirnyi of Belarus won the Wimbledon mixed doubles title. They defeated Mahesh Bhupathi and Mirjana Lucic 6-4, 6-4.

It was now up to Venus to carry on the family name. After Venus beat Chandra Rubin in the third round, she faced Ruano-Pascual. As she had in the past, Venus took revenge on her sister's previous opponent. "I wanted to win every point, all the points that Serena couldn't win yesterday." Volleying with authority and showing an all-court game, she beat Virginia Ruano-Pascual 6-3,6-1.

Venus was playing so well, she looked like a real title threat. Venus said Wimbledon would be the ideal place to win her first Grand Slam title. "It all starts right now... I'm trying to get as serious as possible. I want to have every point. The people that win the Slams are the people who work the hardest." There was still another lesson for Venus to learn. The players who win the slams are the ones who keep their cool. Venus didn't.

A series of calls that went against Venus fired up her, and then the crowd. First there was chair umpire Mike Morrisey's overrule of a set-point called wide on a forehand by Novotna. Venus let that go without an argument, won the next point, but wound up losing the game and set.

With Williams serving to start the second set, a lineswoman signaled good on a groundstroke by Novotna that appeared long and wide. Though Williams stayed with the ball and eventually won the rally, she furiously charged over afterward to shout at Morrisey: "That was SO far out."

Getting no satisfaction there, Williams marched over to the lineswoman, stood over her, inches from her face, and screamed. When that confrontation ended, Williams went back to serve and lost the game immediately on a Novotna volley.

Later, she really lost her temper over another non-call. Pointing and screaming at chair umpire Mike Morrissey she screeched, "I know it's out, She (Novotna) knows it's out. Everybody here knows it's out!" She stated pointing her index finger at the crowd. "Only you don't know it's out." Williams was angry and crying. It was the first time the 18-year-old Williams had lost her temper so badly in a match.

When she double-faulted to lose the game, falling behind 4-3, Williams was shaking and crying on the changeover. Her mood calmed and she fought to send the second set to a tiebreaker. But Williams lost the final five points, smacking forehands into the net on three of them.

Venus was much calmer after the match. Of the disputed line calls, she claimed she had to argue. "I felt like I needed to do that because I really wanted to win those points, and the ball was really out," she said. ". . . But you have to learn to get through those things. I was probably pretty loud, though."

Said Novotna: "I think she lost it there a little bit for a while. Maybe she had a good reason for that, but that (bad calls) happens to everybody."

Later, Williams laughed about the entertainment value of her tantrums. "I think the crowd probably enjoyed my emotional outbursts," she said. "I guess someone would turn the channel and suddenly see some girl screaming and keep it there. I know I would. It probably brightened up someone's day." The need for emotional maturity was just one more lesson Venus was learning.

Venus had mixed success for the rest of 1998. In August, she lost to Lindsay Davenport in the finals of the Bank of the West Classic. Soon after, with her left knee again acting up, she withdrew in the quarter-finals of the Toshiba Classic while playing Mary Pierce. She didn't even try to play in the Acura Classic the following week.

In September, Venus was well-rested for the U.S. Open in New York, the site of her rise to tennis fame just one year earlier. She brought seven different tennis dresses with her, expecting to play seven matches including the championship. She only got to wear six. She lost to Lindsay Davenport in the semi-finals.

"I'm deeply saddened I didn't have the opportunity to wear my seventh dress," she said afterward. "It was red, white and blue matching my hair and nails. I'm definitely going to put that one in a coffin and bury it."

Venus was finding out it was easier to get to the top five, than it was to rise higher to four, three, two and the cherished number one spot. "I really have to work harder on being better," she said after her loss in the U.S. Open. "I played OK but I have to keep on improving. That's all you can do."

And improve she did. In October she beat Patty Schnyder in the finals of the Grand Slam Cup in Munich, Germany. She won $800,000, just slightly less than the $913,000 she had earned during the previous ten months. She quickly reverted, though, losing early in the Porsche Grand Prix to 12th-ranked Dominique van Roost, and to Lindsay Davenport in the European Indoor finals over the next two weeks.

Venus was nominated for two awards late that year,

Venus and Serena compete together in a doubles match at the Australian Open tournament in January, 1999.

Most Improved Player and Most Exciting Player. But she ended the year though on a down note, withdrawing from the Chase Championships in New York. Her knee was hurting again.

It didn't get Venus down, though. She predicted that she would be number one in 1999. "There is always a place to get better in your game. You can't get to a plateau, you have to keep rising."

In January, 1999, she won the Super-Power challenge Cup in Hong Kong over an ailing Steffi Graf, then lost to Graf a week later in the Adidas International in Sydney,

Australia. Venus had good company in losing to Graf, though. Serena had loss to Steffi in the previous round.

In the first Grand Slam event of the year, the Australian Open, Venus not only lost to Lindsay Davenport again, but also lost a handful of beads which cost her a point. She then lost something else – her temper

Serena follows through on an ace against Lindsay Davenport at the Evert Cup in March, 1999. She upset her opponent 6-4, 6-2.

Venus takes flight while winning the Lipton Championships in March, 1999. Her opponent in this championship match was – sister Serena.

again. Her funk seemed to carry over as she lost to Jana Novotna in the finals of the Hanover WTA Tournament in February.

Things were about to change dramatically, though. For one thing, Venus started to wear her beads further back on her head, to avoid hitting them with her racquet. More importantly, due to semi-secret training with Nick

Bollettieri, who worked with both girls not just on their skills but also on their mental approach, both she and Serena were about to make tennis history.

On February 28, 1999, Serena Williams won her first pro championship and $500,000 at the Paris Open. Serena gave her improved backhand credit for her 6-2 3-6 7-6 win against Amelie Mauresmo of France. Perhaps Mauresmo was tired because of previous matches. But the win was an ecstatic one for Serena, who said, "That's my first title. It was a great match for me and I played very well today. It's fantastic." Maresmo showed good sportsmanship when she remarked, "Serena played brilliant tennis today. I tried everything but she was stronger than me in the tie-break even if it was very close."

Never before had two siblings won championships, not just in tennis but in any sport, on the very same day. After Serena won her first WTA Tour title earlier in the day at the Open Gaz de France in Paris, Venus successfully defended her first pro title by beating Amanda Coetzer of South Africa, 6-4, 6-0, in the final of the IGA Superthrift Tennis Classic in Oklahoma City.

The appearance of Serena in France while Venus was in Oklahoma marked a new strategy for the close-knit sisters. They would try to avoid playing each other in tournaments in the future to lessen strain on the family.

Not so in March, 1999, however. They were both

scheduled to play in the Lipton Championships in Key Biscayne. As it turned out, they weren't finished making tennis history.

Venus reached the finals of the Lipton championships by defeating Steffi Graf. Serena beat Martina Hingis for the first time in her career to earn her slot in the finals. This was the first time two sisters had played each other in a major final since Maude Watson upset her older sister Lilian at Wimbledon in 1884. But, unlike the Watsons who wore billowing white skirts, the Williams sisters strolled onto the court wearing skin-tight designer outfits.

Breaking tennis tradition, they warmed up together to the blaring strains of "We Are Family," though both Williams girls had a lot at stake individually. Venus had her 1998 Lipton title to defend and a 2-0 record against her little sister to uphold, and Serena had her tour-leading 16-match undefeated streak on the line, along with an opportunity to break into the Top 10 if she beat Venus and won the title.

While the two sisters slugged away in the final of the major tournament, their father sat in the stands scribbling with a grease pencil on his white message board. His first sign aptly said, "Welcome to the Williams show."

Venus defeated Serena, 6-1, 4-6, 6-4. The match ended when Serena's forehand shot clipped the net and caromed wide. Venus didn't jump, cheer, pump her fists or do her normal victory dance. She just stood there, and so did Serena. Then they slowly walked towards each other, and exchanged a high-five at the net. As they walked toward the umpire's chair, Venus draped her arm around her sister, gently patted her shoulder and whispered into her ear. They walked off as if they were just leaving practice.

Afterwards, Serena said, "I can't say that our relationship is going to be affected by tennis. We have a strong background. We really believe that family comes first, not a game that's going to last 10 years at the most. Why would I want that to come between someone who has always been around, always been a very special friend for me? I couldn't imagine that, and I don't think she could either."

Said Venus, "In the end, we go home, we live life. You have to remind yourself that it's a game, and there's only one winner."

Their nearly two hour match over, many tennis experts said it was only the first of what promises to be a lengthy sister-to-sister rivalry, that this final would only be the first of many. Steffi Graf, whose last three losses had been to one or the other Williams sister, said the duo are destined for great things. "Their athleticism is incredible, they're taking risks, they don't really have a certain weakness, and they're tall and big," Graf said.

Perhaps no one believes it more than their father, who had been predicting tennis greatness since they were little girls in the ghetto. During the match, one of his signs simply said, "I told you so."

*****

Still more good things were to happen in the Spring of 1999. In June, the Williams sisters again made tennis history. The duo defeated Martina Hingis and Anna Kournikova for the doubles title at the French Open. It was the first time sisters had won a doubles title in a Grand Slam event in the history of tennis. It also was the first doubles loss for Martina after seven straight titles.

As Venus and Serena mature and become more comfortable in the pro ranks, their relationships with the other players are improving. Even Irina Spirlea has made peace. "I think they've changed a lot," she said after the Lipton. "Now we can start making jokes, and they can handle it. They are normal now."

Although the girls grew up in a rough neighborhood, today, due to their successes in tennis, the Williams family compound in Florida consists of a modest-sized white home with a satellite dish, several garages, and an assortment of riding lawnmowers and cars both new and old. There is a covered cement deck adjacent to a red hard court that has "Williams" emblazoned in huge white letters across its green backdrop.

The sisters love to be at home and love the family dogs, Star, Queen and Chase. The beach is only twenty minutes away from the Williams home, and Venus and

Serena love to go there and surf. They've kept up their interests in books and learning, including private tutors; even practice partner Gerard Gdebey helped teach them French.

The girls have always displayed a maturity beyond their years on and off the court. Women's tennis analyst Pam Shriver recalled an incident that surprised her and left a lasting impression. "I ran into [Venus] at the Cincinnati airport and she was with her sister, Serena, at the bookstore. I'm thinking to myself, 'In what bunch of books is Venus looking?' They were looking at the classical and poetry section. I was like, 'WOW. There aren't many 17-year-old tennis players I know that would go right to that section, if they would have stepped into the bookstore at all.'"

Although Venus and Serena are rising to the top, they both realize that could change quickly. Both suffer from knee problems which could shorten their playing days. So, the two have developed other interests. Serena has said she would someday like to be a vet and Venus would like to be a fashion designer. "There are so many things that I want to do that are more creative like designing clothes," says Venus. "Not runway fashions. I'm more into clothes for average people."

Her mother, noting how unemotional Venus is when she loses, agrees. "I think Venus wants to do other things," she has said.

Then there's the lure of Hollywood. Both girls have

taken screen tests and received high marks for their charm and charisma. It's possible someday we may see the Williams girls in the movies.

For now, it's tennis. It's more than likely Venus and Serena will be making headlines in the sport for years to come. If not, with their education, faith and family support, you can be sure they will excel at whatever they choose to do.

Bibliography

Books

Mewshaw, Michael; "Ladies of the Court" (New York: Crown Publishers, 1993).

Teitelbaum, Michael; "Grand Slam Stars" (New York: Harper-Collins, 1998).

Periodicals

Associated Press: August 29, 1997; January 22, 1998; March 25, 1998; May 22, 1998; May 23, 1998; May 26, 1998; June 16, 1998; June 17, 1998; June 19, 1998; June 25, 1998; June 28, 1998; June 29, 1998; June 30, 1998.

Atlanta Journal-Constitution: January 27, 1998; February 1, 1998; February 7, 1997; March 5, 1998; March 29, 1998; June 6, 1998.

Baltimore Sun: October 23, 1993.

Business Week: September 29, 1997.

CBS Sportsline: September 5, 1997; September 7, 1997; January 13, 1998; January 14, 1998; June 25, 1998; June 26, 1998; June 29, 1998; July 2, 1998; July 5, 1998; July 6, 1998.

Christian Science Monitor: September 4, 1997; May 22, 1998.

CNN/SI: August 22, 1997; September 10, 1997.

Cosmopolitan: February, 1998.

Ebony: May, 1995; November, 1997; January, 1998.

Emerge: June, 1997.

Jet: September 29, 1997; February 9, 1998.

Just Sports For Women: May, 1998.

Ladies Home Journal: January, 1998.

Life: January, 1998.

Los Angeles Times: July 1, 1998.

New York Times: April 8, 1991; January 13, 1992; April 6, 1992; May 21, 1992; October 22, 1993; November 10, 1993; November 21, 1993; August 26, 1997; September 7, 1997; November 3, 1998.

New York Times Magazine: May 26, 1996; March 16, 1997; June 27, 1997.

Newsday: September 7, 1997.

Newsweek: September 12, 1994.

Palm Beach Post: October 4, 1994; October 5, 1994; November 2, 1994; February 19, 1995; July 19, 1995; August 27, 1996; September 15, 1996; November 15, 1996; March 24, 1997; May 27, 1997; June 27, 1997; August 3, 1997; September 1, 1997; September 5, 1997; September 7, 1997; September 8, 1997; September 12, 1997; September 26, 1997; October 23, 1997; January 20, 1998; January 21, 1998; January 26, 1998; January 28, 1998; February, 24, 1998; February 25, 1998; February 27, 1998; February 28, 1998; March 2, 1998; March 8, 1998; March 10, 1998; March 20, 1998; March 21, 1998; March 22, 1998; March 23, 1998; March 29, 1998; May 6, 1998; May 8, 1998; May 11, 1998; May 24, 1998; May 28, 1998; June 3, 1998; June 17, 1998; July 6, 1998.

People: October 27, 1997; December 29, 1997.

Philadelphia Inquirer: November 10, 1997; January 20, 1998.

Reuters: June 15, 1995; August 25, 1997; March 1, 1998.

Seventeen Magazine: April, 1996; July, 1998.

Sport Magazine: February, 1995.

Sporting News: July 2, 1998.

Sports Illustrated: June 10, 1991; June 13, 1994; November 14, 1994; May 29, 1995; June 28, 1997; July 7, 1997; September 15, 1997; November 17, 1997.

Tennis Magazine: February, 1994; April, 1994; August, 1994; January, 1995; July, 1995; August, 1995; May, 1997; July, 1997; September, 1997; January, 1998; February, 1998.

Young Superstars of Tennis

USA Weekend: April 12, 1998.
Village Voice: September 16, 1997.
Vogue: May, 1998.
Washington Post: September 3, 1997; September 6, 1997; September 8, 1997; January 4, 1998; January 22, 1998.

Glossary

Ace: When a player serves and the opponent is unable to touch the ball with his racquet to return it.

Advantage: The game point following deuce. If a player wins the "advantage" point, he or she wins the game.

Approach Shot: A shot played with the aim of winning a point quickly, often hit from mid-court deep into the corner of the opponent's court. The attacking player normally goes to the net to intercept any return with a volley.

Backhand: A type of stroke. When the ball is hit with the 'back side' of the racquet. The player will have to cross his body with the hand holding the racquet. If a player is right-handed, then a shot hit on the left side of the player's body would be a backhand.

Backspin: Where the ball is hit in a way that makes it spin backwards during flight. Also known as slice.

Baseline: The line at the back of the court. A player stands at the baseline to serve. When both players stand at or behind the baseline to hit the ball back and forth to each other, this is referred to as a 'baseline rally'.

Baseline Tennis: A playing strategy where a player remains at the baseline and attempt to wear their opponents down through long rallies, or -- should the opportunity arise -- to win the point with a passing shot.

Best of Three (or Five): Refers to the maximum number of sets in any match. In "best of three" matches, players need to win two of the three sets.

Break (of service): Where the serving player loses the game. For example; Player A is serving to Player B. If Player B wins the game, Player B has 'broken the serve' of Player A.

Breakpoint: Player A is serving to Player B. Player B needs only one more point to win the game. This is breakpoint. Player A is serving and the score is 30-40. Player A has 30, Player B has 40. Player B needs only one more point to win the game. Player B has 'break point'.

Bye: Free pass into the second round of a tournament. Players may be given a bye if a tournament doesn't have an equal number of players for opening matches. Byes are always awarded to seeded players.

Center Mark: A mark halfway across the baseline, effectively the extension of the center line. When serving, players must remain on the correct side of this mark.

Change of Ends: The players change ends of the court after every "uneven" game (1,3,5) in a set.

Chop: Backspin, defensive shot used to return fast services. Occasionally also used for drop shots.

Cross Shot or Crosscourt: A stroke played diagonally across the court, either long or short. Long cross shots are usually played from baseline to baseline, while short cross shots generally bounce near the opponent's service court line, often being played with topspin.

Deuce: The score in a game where both players have forty points.

Drive: A powerful stroke with slight topspin. Given its long, straight trajectory it is well-suited as a passing shot or attempted winner.

Drop Shot: When a player hits the ball softly so that it just clears the net and falls softly on the opponents court. The ball barely bounces up. By hitting a drop shot, the opponent generally doesn't have enough time to run up to the net to get to the ball.

Double Fault: A situation where the server has failed to serve correctly on both the first and second serve. The server loses the point.

Flat Serve: A flat service is hit without spin and follows a low, straight trajectory. Given the high risk of hitting the net, it is generally better-suited for first serves.

Foot Fault: An error occurring when a player steps onto or over the baseline, sideline or the center mark when serving. Foot faults also occur if the player fails to serve from a static position.

Forehand: A ground stroke played by left-handers to the left of the body, and by right-handers to the right.

Game Part of a Set: Every set consists of at least six games.

Game point: The point needed to win a game.

Grip: The way a player holds the racquet in his hand. Also refers to the wrapping around the handle of the racquet.

Ground Strokes: A type of stroke used to hit the ball after it has bounced. Generally groundstrokes are hit by a player from the baseline. The forehand and backhand are the two types of groundstrokes. When a groundstroke is used, the ball generally travels from baseline to baseline.

Half-court: The area halfway from the baseline to the net. The bottom of the service box is the half-court line. Generally used to describe where a player is standing when a shot is hit.

Inside-out: Type of shot in which the player hits the ball away from his body in a wide angle to the opponent's corner, can be either a forehand or backhand.

Let: An point which has to be replayed. Occurs most frequently when a serve touches the net but still lands in the correct service court.

Lob: A lob is a ball hit in a high arc, usually over the opponent's head. For the most part it is played when the opponent is standing at the net.

Love: "No score" in tennis is announced as "love." It is believed saying this has its origin in the French language. Tennis dates back to 18th-century France. Nil, or nothing, is numerically zero, and the shape of a zero resembles that of an egg. French tennis players adopted their word for egg - l'oeuf - to announce "no score." When tennis began being played in Great Britain, the English pronounced l'oeuf as "love." For example, love-thirty = 0-30.

Match point: The score where a player only needs one more point to win the match.

Net: The device strung up at the middle of the court that the ball is hit over. Can also be a verb meaning to hit the ball into the net.

Overhead: A shot hit when the ball is high overhead, similar to a serve. Generally used when the opponent tries to I lob, but the ball isn't hit high or far enough. A player will counter-act by hitting an overhead, sometimes referred to as an overhead smash, or simply, smash.

Passing Shot: A groundstroke that an opponent located close to the net is unable to intercept and return. It's usually hit down the line or cross court. Ball actually passes the opponent who is rushing the net, standing at half court or standing at the net.

Player Rankings: The WTA computer ranking system started in January 1997, tabulating player points each week. According to the WTA, the new ranking system's goal was to "strengthen fields at worldwide tournaments to enable fans to see top players play each other more often. This would build intriguing rivalries and even greater excitement in women's tennis." The more you play and win matches, the higher your ranking. The less you play or lose matches, the lower your ranking.

Racquet: Device used by a player to hit the ball. Comes in various sizes (Oversize, Midsize, Extended) and brands (Wilson, Prince)

Rally: A series of shots hit back and forth between two players.

Return of Serve: Shot hit by a player in response to opponent's serve. If Player A is serving to Player B and Player B hits a shot that Player A is unable to play, Player B has hit "a return of serve winner."

Rushing the Net: The action by which a player runs towards the net in an attempt to play an aggressive style of tennis.

Serve or Service: Every point begins with a serve. From a position behind the baseline, the server has to hit the ball diagonally over the net into the opponent's service court. Players get two attempts to serve the ball. In the first point of any game or set, the serve is played from the right-hand side of the court. After this the server moves to the other side then alternates side at the start of every new point.

Serve and Volley: A tactic where players serve and then rush to the net with the aim of playing a winning volley off the opponent's return.

Service Lines: The service line runs parallel to the net. Together with the center line and sideline, it marks the boundaries of the service courts.

Service Winner: When a player serves a ball that is touched by the opponent, but is not returned, hence a winner by serve. Since the ball was touched by the opponent, it is not an ace.

Set: A set comprises at least six games. Matches are generally played over three or five sets.

Set Point: The point needed to win a set.

Slice: A slice shot differs from a "drive" in that the backspin applied keeps it in the air for longer, causing it to travel further before bouncing.

Slice Serve:: Side spin and topspin are applied to the serve, causing the ball to keep low and change direction after bouncing. Slice serves from right-handed players cut sharply away to the left.

Smash: Another word for an overhead hit very forcefully.

Spin: The rotation of a ball resulting from special types of strokes like slice and topspin. Spin affects a ball's flight and the way it bounces.

Tie-break Rule: Used for deciding sets where the score has reached 6-6. During tie-breaks players are awarded points numerically. The first player with 7 points wins the set, provided he or she has a lead of 2 points, such as 7-5. If not, play continues until there is a two-point advantage lead, 10-8, for example. The score for the set is then recorded as 7-6, (seven games to six).

Topspin: A stroke where the player hits the top surface of the ball, causing it to rotate forwards.

Umpire: The umpire decides which player has won a point and also keeps the score. In major tournaments the umpire is assisted by a number of judges.

Unforced Error: An mistake made while under no pressure from the opponent, such as mishitting a ball.

USTA: United States Tennis Association.

Volley: A type of shot that is hit while standing close to the net. The ball is hit before it bounces with a short, punching motion.

Winner: A shot the opponent cannot return.

WTA: Women's Tennis Association.

Young Superstars of Tennis

HOW TENNIS IS PLAYED

The server delivers the ball from behind the baseline. Two tries are permitted for each service. If the ball strikes any part of the opponent's court except the service box, a "fault" is called. A fault is also called if the ball is served into the net, or if it strikes the net before hitting the opponent's court outside the service box.

After a successful serve the ball is hit back and forth until one player or side fails to return the ball successfully. A shot is unsuccessful when a player lets the ball bounce twice, hits it into the net, or hits it beyond the boundaries of the opposite side of the court.

HOW TENNIS IS SCORED

Scoring is identical in singles and doubles games. A game is played to four points, designated as 15, 30, 40 and Game. A tie at 40 is called "deuce." A game must be won by two points.

A player must win six games to win a set, but he must win by at least two games. A tiebreaker is often used if the set is tied 6-6. Tiebreakers are generally played to 7 points, and the winner must win the tiebreaker by at least two points. Tennis matches are usually two sets out of three or three sets out of five.

PLAYING SURFACES

Tennis can be played on grass, clay or on hard surfaces, like those found on most public courts. Grass is said to be a "fast" surface, while clay is "slow." Hard courts – such as DecoTurf and Rebound Ace are "medium."

The surfaces at the four Grand Slam events are red clay in Paris, grass at Wimbledon, DecoTurf at the U.S. Open and Rebound Ace at the Australian Open.

The Venus and Serena Williams Story

The speed of a tennis surface is determined by how much time it allows a player to hit the ball. Grass is said to be fast because the ball slashes through low and hard after landing, giving players little time to react. Clay, because the ball bounces high after hitting a forgiving and gritty surface, is considered slow.

Aggressive, serve-and-volley players like grass because they can move forward to the net knowing their opponents will have little time to counter-attack. Baseliners, who are more comfortable from the backcourt, prefer clay because it gives them time to hit their ground strokes without feeling rushed.

DIFFERENCES IN SURFACES

Clay

Unlike the other surfaces, the ball leaves a mark when it hits a clay surface. Also, The half-inch clay - which is really crushed brick, shale or stone - is soft and moisture-absorbent. This allows players to slide into their shots. There are red and green clay courts.

Grass

Lawn tennis was the sport's name at the first Wimbledon in 1877, and lawn tennis it remains today. The Wimbledon courts are a combination of rye grass and creeping red fescue. They're cut short and, depending on the weather, may be mowed, rolled and watered every day. The ball skids through low on the greasy grass, making conditions fast. If there isn't too much rain, the grass wears and the ground hardens making playing conditions slower.

Hard Surfaces

DecoTurf's surface is made up of a number of different materials including rubber particles. The court's speed depends on an acrylic latex topping that can be smooth (fast) or textured (slower).

Rebound Ace is more cushioned than DecoTurf, the result of a thick rubber base made from recycled tires. Two applications of acrylic coating are the last of 10 thin layers that top off Rebound Ace courts. The surface can be a bit spongy on hot, sunny days, resulting in a higher bounce.

Index